edexcel
advancing learning, changing lives

Edexcel AS History Unit 1
Pursuing Life and Liberty: Equality in the USA 1945–1968

Robin Bunce and Laura Gallagher
Series editors: Derrick Murphy and Angela Leonard

STUDENT BOOK

A PEARSON COMPANY

Contents

Introduction

Welcome to History at AS level. History is a fascinating subject, concerned with the world as it was and how it became the world we know now. By studying history, you will encounter new people, new places, new societies and cultures – even though they are all in the past! If you have an enquiring mind and an interest in the world around you then History is the subject for you.

How to make the most of the course

- Practise your skills. History is not just about learning information or about telling the story of what happened in the past. You need to be able to understand and explain why things turned out the way they did and about how much they changed. The Skills Builder sections in this book will help you do this.

- Prepare for debate and discussion. Historians do not always agree about why events or developments in the past happened, or about their importance – so don't be afraid to debate with your teacher and other students. But remember that you must give evidence to support any point you make.

- Use the course book. This book has been designed to help you build up the skills, knowledge and understanding to help you do well in your exam – so use it! See the 'How this book will help you' section overleaf for details.

- Read around the subject. The more you learn about a period of history, the more interesting it becomes. Further reading on your chosen topics will broaden your understanding of the period, give you better insights into causation and change, and make the course much more rewarding.

What you will learn

Unit 1 focuses on historical themes in breadth. This means that you need to be able to understand and explain why things changed over a fairly long period. In Option D5 you will learn about the struggle by black people in the USA for equal rights between 1945 and 1968. You will study the forms of racial discrimination in America at the time, and the methods used by black Americans to challenge this discrimination. You will find out about the civil rights leader Martin Luther King and his peaceful protest campaigns. You will examine the extent to which the federal government aided the civil rights campaigners, and the extent to which opposition was effective in preventing civil rights. In addition, you will consider why the Black Power movement adopted more militant forms of protest. Finally, you will put these changes in their historical context, considering the development of a wider protest movement in 1960s America, and the impact of the civil rights movement on other ethnic minorities.

How you will be assessed

For Unit 1 you will take a written exam. You will write two essays: one on each topic you have studied (i.e. one on the civil rights movement and one on your other chosen topic). For each topic you will have a choice of two questions. You will have 1 hour and 20 minutes in total, or 40 minutes for each essay.

How this book will help you

- Clearly written text gives you the historical information you need for this topic in the right amount of depth.

- 'Take note' boxes indicate when you should make notes of your own. These notes will help you with the activities and can also form the basis of your revision, so it's worth keeping up to date with these as you go along.

- Activities help you understand the content and build up your historical skills.

- Skills builder sections help you develop the essential skills you need to do well in your exam.

- Examzone tells you what you need to know to prepare for the exam, including:

  — what to expect on the day

  — how to revise

  — what the assessment objectives mean and how you can meet them

  — what the different levels mean and how you can gain a high mark

  — example essays with examiner commentaries to help you understand what the examiners are looking for and how to use your information.

Chapter 1   **From slavery to segregation**

Key questions

- How did American society become segregated?
- What were the effects of racism in the northern and the southern states?

African American Jesse Owens was the finest athlete at the 1936 Olympic Games. He won four gold medals in the 100 metres, 200 metres, long jump and 100 metres relay. His achievement was highly political. Owens was a black man and the Olympics took place in Nazi Germany. Hitler, the Nazi leader, believed that black people were inferior and refused to shake his hand.

But that was not the only racism that Owens experienced. When he returned to America he was invited to attend a celebration of his success in his home town in Alabama. The crowd applauded Owens, but then he was asked to leave. As a black man he was not allowed to share the celebration dinner with the white people of the town. The best athlete in the world was a second-class citizen in his own town because of the colour of his skin.

Timeline

1787	American Constitution drafted
1791	Bill of Rights added to the American Constitution
1861–1865	American Civil War
1862	Emancipation Proclamation
1865	Thirteenth Amendment: slavery abolished
1868	Fourteenth Amendment: citizenship guaranteed for all races
1870	Fifteenth Amendment: voting rights guaranteed for all races
1890–1910	'Jim Crow' laws passed across the southern states of America
1896	*Plessy v. Ferguson*: US Supreme Court allows the policy of racial segregation

Slavery – America's 'original sin'

Barack Obama, America's first **black** President, described slavery as America's 'original sin'. By this, he meant that slavery was a fundamental wrong that oppressed black people from the earliest days of America's history. The first black slaves were brought to America in the early seventeenth century, where most of them were used to work on farms in the southern states. They grew and harvested crops such as cotton and tobacco.

The **American Revolution** created an independent country in which all of its citizens enjoyed legally protected rights. However, these rights did not extend to the vast majority of American blacks, who still had the status of slaves. Slavery was an institution in which one human being became the property of another. Slaves had no rights whatsoever. They could be treated in whatever way their owner saw fit.

Take note

The information in this chapter can be divided into three periods: slavery, reconstruction and segregation.
Copy the table below. As you read, complete it for each of these periods.

Period	Situation for African Americans
Slavery	
Reconstruction	
Segregation	

Glossary:

Black

Americans of African descent have been described by a variety of terms. Although the terms Negro and colored were widely used from 1945 to 1968, this book uses black and African American, which are widely used today.

Source 1.1: Barack Obama describes the limits of American democracy

Democratic debate might have been sufficient to give the right to vote to white men and eventually women. But debate alone could not provide the slave his freedom or cleanse America of its original sin.
Taken from: *The Audacity of Hope* by Barack Obama (2007)

Glossary:

North and South

Throughout this book, these are general terms that distinguish between the states with legal segregation (the South) and those without (the North). It was not a hard-and-fast geographical distinction: some segregated states were further north than the 'northern' states.

Emancipation

The act of liberating (freeing) a person from another's control.

The American Revolution and civil war

This won independence for America from the British Empire. The American civil war, almost a century later, was a battle between Americans about the type of country they wanted to live in.

By the nineteenth century, slavery had been abolished throughout America's northern states, but it continued across the **South**. America consists of a number of states, each of which has its own government. In the eighteenth and nineteenth centuries, these states had considerable independence and therefore it was possible for laws to differ significantly between states. Slavery was one of the central reasons for the outbreak of **civil war** between the 'slave states' of the South and the 'free states' of the North. American President Abraham Lincoln, who led the northern states, declared the freedom of all American slaves in his 1862 **Emancipation** Proclamation. Following the North's victory in the civil war in 1865, slavery was finally abolished across America. This was achieved by passing the Thirteenth Amendment to the American Constitution, which made slavery illegal.

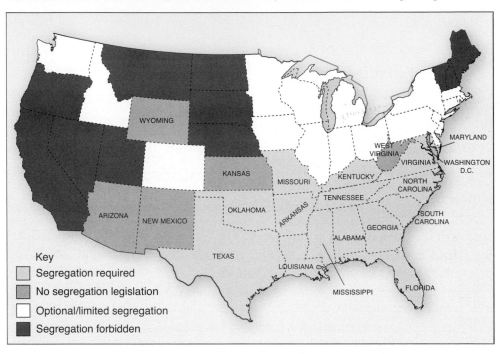

Key
- Segregation required
- No segregation legislation
- Optional/limited segregation
- Segregation forbidden

Between 1890 and 1950 segregation was imposed to varying degrees across the American states. The map shows the variation by 1950.

The American Constitution and political system

The American Constitution is a document written in 1787 and adopted in 1788 that defines the rights, duties and structure of government in America. The Bill of Rights – an addition to the Constitution in 1791 – sets out the freedoms that all American citizens should enjoy.
America is a federal system, in which individual states have their own governments which make and enforce local laws. Above state government is the national – or federal – government, which is responsible for creating and enforcing laws that apply throughout the whole of America. America's national laws are made by Congress, a body which is similar to the British Parliament. The President is the head of the American government, but is not all-powerful as he or she has to work with Congress in order to pass laws.
The government's powers are limited by the rights that American citizens enjoy. If the government denies a citizen their rights, then the citizen can take the government to court and force the government to back down. Indeed, America's Supreme Court has the power to declare government action illegal and even to strike down laws that breach the freedoms set out in the Bill of Rights.

Reconstruction

In the 25 years following the American Civil War (1861–1865), attempts were made to make America a fairer society and to rebuild the southern states. During this period, which is known as reconstruction, two further **constitutional amendments** were passed in an attempt to give African Americans the rights they had been denied for so long.

- The Fourteenth Amendment (1868) gave citizenship rights to all people born in the United States of America and was an attempt to guarantee the rights of the people who had formerly been slaves.

- The Fifteenth Amendment (1870) gave all citizens voting rights regardless of their race.

These legal rights were never fully enforced, although some progress was made towards racial equality, even in the South.

Segregation: Re-imposing white supremacy in the South

A belief in **white supremacy** was particularly entrenched in the southern states. The end of slavery had been a blow to white supremacy. However, southern racists were able to devise new ways of oppressing black people.

'Jim Crow' laws

Between 1890 and 1910, southern states introduced legal **segregation**. This was achieved by passing local laws which denied black Americans access to facilities used by white Americans. These laws were known as the '**Jim Crow**' laws. For example, education, healthcare, transport, and public facilities more generally, were segregated. This included restaurants, cinemas, toilets, bus stations and drinking fountains.

Source 1.2: George Kenneth Butterfield Junior describes his hometown in North Carolina

We basically had two local black physicians. Each had his own practice. Their medical resources were limited. There was only one black hospital, called Mercy Hospital, which was understaffed and underfunded and just second-rate. Nevertheless, that was the only hospital for black citizens. Back then there were no ambulances. If you needed to get to a hospital in an emergency situation, you would call the funeral home. I saw a case one time where a white funeral home was called and they got to the scene and found out it was a black patient. They turned around and went back. They did not give any assistance.
Taken from: *Remembering Jim Crow*, eds. Chafe, Gavins and Korstadt (2001)

'The segregated heart'

Segregation was not just a legal matter. It was also an attitude of mind which governed even the smallest aspects of behaviour, including how people stood, sat, ate, walked and made eye contact. Sarah Patton Boyle, who grew up in Virginia in the 1910s, described this as a 'racial etiquette'. By this she meant that there were unspoken rules which governed the way that black and white people related to each other. As a young white woman she learned to talk down to local blacks. For example, whites never called black men 'Mr' or black women 'Mrs'. Equally, black people were never invited into a white

Take note

Complete the following spider diagram, using information from the section 'Segregation: Re-imposing white supremacy in the South'.
It is important that you create a summary of the information in this section in the table mentioned on page 5. In order to make more detailed notes, complete the following spider diagram.

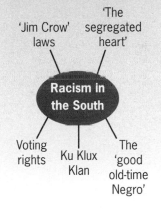

Glossary:
Disenfranchise

Remove someone's right to vote.

Stereotype

Description of a group of things or people that attributes certain, often negative, characteristics to all members of the group.

Lynching

The illegal execution of someone by a mob, usually by hanging.

family's dining room, but they could eat together in the kitchen or on the back porch. By the age of three of four, black and white children had already learned how to relate to each other so that white superiority and black inferiority were consistently asserted. Boyle described this as 'segregation of the heart'.

Voting rights

Under the Fifteenth Amendment, black people had the legal right to vote throughout America. Nonetheless, the southern states found devious ways to **disenfranchise** the local black population. For example, some states introduced a 'grandfather clause' which meant that people could only vote if their grandfathers had been able to vote. Other states introduced literacy tests as criteria for voting. Literacy tests were not applied fairly and therefore even educated black people were disenfranchised. These were not explicitly racist, but both prevented black Americans from voting.

The 'good, old-time negro'

Although the southern states were segregated, white people often relied on black people for domestic help. Black people were hired to bring up white children, to cook, to clean and to provide nursing care for rich white people. As a result, black and white people often had intimate relationships, and white people were dependent on the skills of their black employees. Many rich whites therefore had contradictory feelings about black Americans. They saw them as an 'inferior race' that should be kept at a distance, and yet they needed them in their family lives. In order to make this situation easier, white people invented the **stereotype** of the 'good old-time negro'. This presented black people as happy to serve white people and entirely satisfied with their role in a segregated society. White people encouraged their black employees to behave in this way by employing black people who seemed to fit in with the stereotype and denying employment to those with higher aspirations.

The Ku Klux Klan

The most radical expression of white supremacy was the Ku Klux Klan. The Klan was an organisation which saw itself as the defender of the white supremacist traditions of the South. The Klan targeted black people who showed any sign of disrespect towards white people. This included black people who were romantically involved with white people, black people who were growing prosperous, and black people who were challenging the injustice of segregation. The Klan terrorised such people by **lynching** their victims. In 1900, there were 115 instances of lynching throughout America. Notably, in the same year, the total number of murders across the United States was only 230.

Between 1915 and 1929, the Klan was extraordinarily powerful. Senior politicians in southern states were often members of the Klan, as were judges, policemen, and other local officials. As a result there was little justice for African Americans in the southern states.

Hooded Klansmen parade through the streets of Long Branch, New Jersey, 4 July 1924.

For many in the South, those in the Klan were heroes. This interpretation of the Klan was promoted in the 1915 film *Birth of a Nation* in which Klansmen are portrayed protecting vulnerable women from local black men. This film was the most popular film of the year and grossed $10 million (the equivalent of about $220 million today).

Challenging segregation in the South

Black people were deeply unhappy with life in the South, and many were prepared to challenge segregation.

Plessy v. Ferguson, 1896

One method of challenging segregation was to go to court and show that 'Jim Crow' laws violated the American Constitution and were therefore illegal. **Homer Plessy** did just this in a landmark case of 1896. Plessy claimed that segregation was unlawful because all citizens were guaranteed equal rights under the Fourteenth Amendment. Consequently, he claimed that the state of Louisiana had acted illegally when they had arrested him for sitting in a white-only area of a railway train.

Homer Plessy

(1863–1925)

Homer Plessy was born in New Orleans in 1863. He was chosen to fight racial segregation by the Citizens' Committee of New Orleans in 1896 because even though he was classified as black, he was seven-eighths white and therefore had a pale skin colour. Notably, the Citizens' Committee tipped off the authorities, who might otherwise have overlooked the violation due to Plessy's appearance.

Take note

As you read through the next section, make two lists:
a) Ways in which black people in the North had a better life than black people in the South.
b) Types of discrimination faced by black people in the North.

Glossary:

Activist

Somebody who fights for a cause.

Ghettoisation

The isolation of a group of people, often of one race, in a specific area within a city, generally with relatively poor facilities.

Plessy took his case to America's Supreme Court. However, the judges decided that segregation was lawful as long as black and white citizens had access to facilities that were equally good. *Plessy v. Ferguson* was highly influential because it laid the legal foundation for segregation. Prior to the Supreme Court's decision, segregation had been spreading fairly slowly. However, once the Supreme Court announced that it was legal to treat people in a way that was 'separate but equal', 'Jim Crow' laws were enforced across the whole of the South.

Conditions in the North

Conditions for black people were quite different in the North.

- There was little legally enforced segregation in the northern states.
- Whereas in the South the majority of blacks worked in agriculture, in the North black people were predominantly industrial workers. Indeed, during the First World War (1914–1918) there was a period known as the 'Great Migration', during which thousands of black Americans moved to the great industrial cities of Chicago and Detroit in order to work in the war industries. The economic boom of the 1920s also attracted blacks to the North – in this period about 500,000 migrated from the southern to the northern states.
- Pay was better in the North, although even there black workers were earning on average only 50 per cent of the pay of white workers.
- Black workers were better organised in the North: in the mid-1920s, black **activist** A. Philip Randolph organised America's first successful black union: the Brotherhood of Sleeping Car Porters.
- Finally, it was easier for black people to vote in the North.

However, black people still faced enormous discrimination in the North and racism was widespread. Additionally, as black people were generally paid less than white people they were forced to live in undesirable neighbourhoods. These areas were often exclusively populated by blacks and had poorer facilities than white areas. Consequently, economic deprivation and **ghettoisation** were substantial problems.

Conclusion

Black Americans faced enormous hardships. Although they were no longer slaves, they were treated as second-class citizens throughout the South and underpaid and forced into ghettos in the North. Nonetheless, there was hope – the American Constitution allowed citizens to challenge unjust laws. Indeed, following the Second World War, black activists would increasingly use legal methods to fight for racial equality.

Activity: Racism on display

Taking it further

In 1920, Oscar Micheaux, an African American film director, released a film entitled *Within Our Gates* as a response to the release of *Birth of a Nation* in 1915. *Within Our Gates* shows the suffering of black Americans due to white oppression in both the North and the South. It is the oldest surviving film by an African American director.

Watch clips from both films, available on the Internet, and contrast the way in which black Americans are portrayed.

Imagine you have been asked to design a museum display about the life of black Americans in the nineteenth century.

Use the Internet to find two pictures to illustrate each of slavery, reconstruction and segregation. Choose pictures that will help visitors understand the topic and write a caption for each one.

You must find:

- two pictures to illustrate slavery

- two pictures to illustrate reconstruction

- four pictures to illustrate segregation.

Once you have chosen the pictures, write captions for them so that a visitor to the museum understands what they reveal about slavery, reconstruction and segregation. You may also wish to use your caption to explain why you chose that picture.

Chapter 2   A divided nation: the position of black Americans in 1945

Key questions

○ In what ways did the Second World War affect the struggle for civil rights?

○ In what ways were conditions different for African Americans in the North and the South in 1945?

○ How far did black Americans share in the economic boom that followed the Second World War?

The American President Franklin Roosevelt presented the Second World War as a 'good war'. Government spin doctors prepared a publicity campaign which portrayed the United States as a democracy fighting for justice and freedom. At the same time, however, American soldiers served in an explicitly racist army. Black soldiers fought in all-black regiments and Asian American soldiers were also segregated.

At home in the USA, African Americans were also fighting for justice and freedom. But this fight was not against the Germans or the Japanese. Rather, they were fighting to overthrow white supremacy in America.

Take note

As you read through the section called *The effects of the Second World War*, make notes about evidence of racism and the progress towards racial equality that occurred during the war. Think about each of the following:

• experience of black soldiers in Europe

• experience of black heroes

• economic changes

• fighting racism during the war.

Glossary:

Radicalised

To make someone more radical – more extreme or unusual in their views or approach.

Timeline

1941	America enters the Second World War Roosevelt establishes the Fair Employment Practices Commission (FEPC)
1943	Detroit Riots William L. Dawson elected to the US Congress
1944	Roosevelt is re-elected American President
1945	The Allies win the Second World War Adam Clayton Powell elected to the US Congress
1949	William Haist appointed a federal judge

The effects of the Second World War on the lives of black Americans

The Second World War was a turning point in America's attitude to race.

Black soldiers in Europe

Over 1.2 million black men joined the United States army during the Second World War. The experience **radicalised** them. Northern blacks were often trained in rural military camps in the southern states. This was their first experience of formal racial segregation. Naturally, they were appalled at the thought that they would be fighting for their country and yet their country treated them as second-class citizens.

Segregation continued during the war. For example, black soldiers had different canteens and were transported to the battlefield in different vehicles from white soldiers, and many were employed as cooks and cleaners, so denied the right to fight. Black soldiers who did make it to the front line were given less training and worse equipment, and in some cases black battalions were sent to the most dangerous parts of the battlefield. Black soldiers were appalled by this treatment and in some cases there were riots in protest.

Black soldiers also experienced European society during their stays in Britain and France. Notably, there was no formal segregation in either country. Furthermore, white people in Europe treated black soldiers as heroes.

African American servicemen enjoying female company on a night out in Germany, 1946.

World War – Race War

Americans were encouraged to support the national effort in the Second World War because the USA and her allies were fighting for a just cause. President Roosevelt argued that America was fighting so that everyone in the world could enjoy four basic freedoms: freedom of speech, freedom of religion, freedom from want, and freedom from fear. Although Roosevelt did not say so explicitly, the implication was that the four basic freedoms applied equally to all people regardless of their race.

Black soldiers were struck by the contradiction of fighting for the four freedoms abroad while they could not enjoy them at home. Consequently, they used the 'Double V' sign, meaning that they were fighting for two victories: victory overseas and victory over racism at home.

Additionally, the United States and her allies were fighting a racist opponent. **Hitler and the Nazis** passionately believed that the 'master race' had the right to enslave and exterminate 'lesser' races. The full horror of what this meant was uncovered in the final phase of the war, when **allied soldiers** liberated Nazi **extermination camps** in Eastern Europe. In the past, organisations such as the Ku Klux Klan had presented racism as something that was both natural and noble. However, the extermination of over six million Jews and other racist atrocities carried out by the Nazis showed the dangers inherent in racism and in so doing convinced many people that racism should be opposed in all circumstances.

Source 2.1: Henry Hooten describes being a black soldier in the American army during the Second World War

Well, I worked up through the ranks. I went in as a private and soon became corporal, and then staff sergeant and first sergeant. It was well segregated. The first trouble I really had was in London. We were getting ready for war. The English people had invited us to a party one night. The people in England was trying to show their appreciation towards us black servicemen. My commander was from Mississippi, and he didn't want his black boys fraternising with white girls in the area. He denied our permission and we couldn't go.

Taken from: *Remembering Jim Crow*, eds. Chafe, Gavins and Korstadt (2001)

Glossary:

Allied soldiers

In the Second World War, allied soldiers, mainly representing the USA, Britain and Russia, fought against Hitler and the Nazis.

Extermination camps

Prison camps designed for mass killings.

The racism of Hitler and the Nazis

Adolf Hitler was the leader of Germany from 1933 to 1945; the Nazis were the ruling political party during this period. The Nazis believed that history was a constant struggle between the master Aryan race, consisting of white Germanic peoples with blond hair, blue eyes and pale skin, and other 'culture-destroying' races, who were considered by the Nazis to be not fully human. The Nazis considered Jews to be the lowest human race.

A. Philip Randolph

(1889–1979)

Pioneering black activist and founder of the Brotherhood of Sleeping Car Porters, a labour union that predominantly represented black workers.

Glossary:
Executive order

An order issued by the President changing the way in which government operates.

Black heroes

The courage of black soldiers fighting in the Second World War changed the attitudes of many white soldiers. For example, in an interview after the war, a platoon sergeant from segregated South Carolina commented:

> 'When I heard about it I said I'd be damned if I'd wear the same shoulder patch they did. After that first day when we saw how they fought I changed my mind. They're just like any of the other boys to us.'

Additionally, fighting in the war boosted the self-esteem of many African Americans. For example, Woodrow Crockett, an American airman, was one of the first black pilots in the American air force. In the last year of the war, he flew 149 missions, protecting European harbours from enemy attack. Not a single plane in the black squadron was ever shot down. Following the war, black heroes who had risked their lives for their country expected recognition for their achievements. They returned determined to challenge racial injustice.

Economic changes

The Second World War transformed the American economy. The government spent vast sums of money creating armaments and supplies for the army. The war economy had a considerable effect on both North and South.

In the South, $4.5 billion was spent creating factories that produced war goods. However, at first black people were unable to get jobs in the booming war industry due to racism on the part of those hiring. Black activist **A. Philip Randolph** was appalled at this 'colour bar'. He threatened to lead a march of African Americans to Washington unless the government forced industries to change. In response, Roosevelt issued an **executive order** creating the Fair Employment Practices Commission (FEPC) in 1941. This forced industries employed in the war effort not to discriminate on the grounds of 'race, creed, colour or national origin' when deciding who to hire. As a result, many black farm workers in the South moved to southern cities in order to get jobs in the new war industries.

Northern industry also boomed, and consequently there was another wave of black migration from South to North. In 1940, approximately a quarter of American blacks lived in the North. They were concentrated in the industrial cities, forming significant minorities of the population in Philadelphia, Detroit, Indianapolis, Chicago and New York. The wartime boom increased migration so, by 1950, almost a third of black Americans lived in the North (see Source 2.2).

Economic changes during the war were significant for black Americans because they allowed them to play a major role in the country's war effort. They were also important because they changed the way in which black Americans lived. By the end of the war, 48 per cent of the black population was urban. Jobs in the cities paid more than those in the country. This change meant that many African Americans were better paid than before. Finally, the campaigning of activists such as A. Philip Randolph showed that putting pressure on the government could force politicians to act in favour of racial equality.

Regional differences following the Second World War: North versus South

By the end of the Second World War, there were clear signs of change for black Americans. However, progress was not equally shared across the United States.

Politics

The Second World War had made some difference to southern politics. For example, before the war less than 2 per cent of the black population in the southern states could vote. By 1945 approximately 15 per cent of the black population of the southern states had been registered to vote. Indeed, in their campaigns to register black voters, civil rights organisations in the South explicitly reminded voters of the fight for freedom and justice in the Second World War and the sacrifices made by black soldiers. Notably, the efforts of black campaigners and black ex-soldiers was greeted with hostility by white racists and there was an increase in the number of lynchings immediately following the war.

In the North, the political power of African Americans was also increasing.

- By 1945 sixteen northern states had black populations that were between 5 and 13 per cent of the total population. In these states, black voters held the balance of power – that is to say, if the black community voted as a block, they could determine the outcome of elections.
- An example of the voting power of African Americans in the North was the election of William L. Dawson (1943) and Adam Clayton Powell, Jr. (1945) to Congress. Dawson and Powell, however, were the only African Americans who were elected to Congress between 1943 and 1955.
- Finally, in recognition of the growing political power of northern blacks, American Presidents began appointing African Americans to positions in the federal government. For example, William Haist was appointed a federal judge in 1949.

Economics

In the southern states, African Americans were still predominantly employed in poorly paid agricultural jobs. However, during the Second World War approximately 500,000 African Americans migrated to the North in search of better conditions and found work in industrial cities such as Chicago, Detroit and San Francisco. There was a threefold rise in the black college population of the northern states. As a result of the war boom, the number of unemployed African Americans fell sharply from 937,000 in 1940 to 151,000 in 1945.

However, even in the North, black industrial workers were unlikely to be paid the same as their white colleagues. Furthermore, white workers

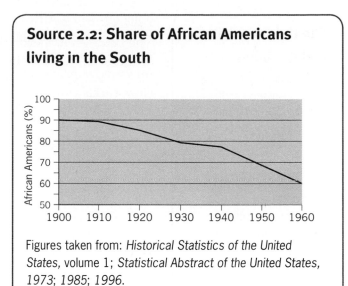

Source 2.2: Share of African Americans living in the South

Figures taken from: *Historical Statistics of the United States*, volume 1; *Statistical Abstract of the United States*, *1973; 1985; 1996.*

Take note

1. As you read through this section, make notes on the political, economic and social differences between the North and South following the Second World War. The notes can be in any form you wish, but remember – the purpose of note-taking is to capture key information in a clear and organised way.
2. Swap notes with a partner. Assess your partner's notes in terms of a) their organisation, b) their clarity, c) their choice of material.
3. List two ways in which your partner could improve their note-taking.

The Detroit riots of 1943

This was a three-day-long and widespread conflict between the black and white citizens of Detroit. The riots led to the deaths of 34 people and the injury of 600 more. Most of those killed or injured were black. The white authorities in the city blamed the riots on black troublemakers. Black leaders, on the other hand, argued that the riot was a response to racial discrimination in terms of jobs and housing as well as ongoing police brutality towards innocent blacks.

objected when African Americans were promoted. For example, the **Detroit riots** of 1943 were highly destructive. Finally, although unemployment had fallen among African Americans, they were still more likely to be unemployed than white Americans. For example, while only 6 per cent of New York's white men were unemployed, the figure was 10 per cent for black men.

Social conditions

At the end of the Second World War, segregation remained throughout the southern states. In Washington D.C., for example, African Americans were barred from all restaurants, cinemas and hotels in the central district of the city. Turning to housing, 40 per cent of housing available to black people in Washington D.C. was found to be sub-standard, whereas only 12 per cent of white housing fell into this category.

The situation was considerably different in the northern states, where eating, transport and educational facilities were not segregated. The absence of segregation meant that the racial etiquette was not as rigid and therefore it was more likely for people from different races to mix. However, the fact that African Americans were poorer than whites meant that they were often forced to live in worse accommodation and in the undesirable parts of cities.

Activity: Spectrum of discrimination

Social conditions for black Americans in the South in 1945

Political conditions for black Americans in the South in 1945

Economic conditions for black Americans in the South in 1945

In the exam, you may be asked a question which begins 'How far…' or 'To what extent…' It can be helpful when considering these questions, to think in terms of a spectrum.

1. Copy the cards on the left.

2. On a large sheet of paper, draw the following spectrum:

⟵——————————————————————————————⟶

'Discriminated against'   'Treated equally'

3. Using the knowledge you have gained from this chapter, place the cards in an appropriate place on the spectrum. Once you have placed your three cards, write next to each card any specific examples that support your conclusions. For example, you may conclude that political conditions for black Americans in the South were highly discriminatory, in which case place the card towards the left of the spectrum. You might write next to the card the example that by 1945 only 15 per cent of southern blacks could vote.

4. Write a paragraph in answer to the question: 'How far do you agree that African Americans were treated as second-class citizens in the southern states between 1940 and 1946?'

Once you have completed this activity, repeat it, but this time consider conditions in the northern states.

Chapter 3   **To Secure These Rights: Truman and the Cold War**

Key questions

- What impact did the Cold War have on the struggle for civil rights?
- Why did Truman seek civil rights reform?
- How successful were Truman's civil rights reforms?

As a young man, Harry S. Truman was racist. He used abusive language, referring to African Americans as 'niggers'. In addition, at the age of 38, he paid $10 to join the Ku Klux Klan. But Truman outgrew his prejudices and became the first American President to publicly challenge segregation, and the first to pledge his support for civil rights.

Timeline

1945	Truman becomes President Beginning of the Cold War
1946	President's Committee on Civil Rights established
1947	*To Secure These Rights* published
1948	Presidential election: Truman re-elected
1951	Committee on Government Contract Compliance (CGCC) established

Take note

As you read through the following sections on Harry S. Truman and the Cold War, list Truman's motivations for addressing black civil rights.

Harry S. Truman – an unexpected reformer

Harry S. Truman was born in the **border state** of Missouri, and as a result experienced segregation first-hand. Truman was undoubtedly racist during his youth. However, he was deeply moved by stories of black war veterans who were the victims of racist attacks after fighting bravely in the Second World War. What is more, Truman was aware of the growing importance of the black vote to the **Democratic Party**. For both of these reasons, Truman became committed to challenging southern racism.

Traditionally, African Americans had supported the **Republican Party**. This was because slavery had ended during the presidency of the Republican Abraham Lincoln (1861–1865). However, because of the popularity of President Roosevelt, black voters had supported the Democrats in large numbers in the 1930s and 1940s, and Truman hoped that this trend would continue if the Democrats backed civil rights.

The impact of the Cold War

The **Cold War** had a significant impact on Truman's commitment to civil rights. Truman believed that America had a moral duty to fight Communism

Democratic Party and Republican Party

The Democrats and the Republicans are America's two main political parties.

The Cold War

An ideological and economic conflict between communist Russia and capitalist America that began following the Second World War. Although it is called a 'war', the two sides never directly fought each other.

Glossary:

Border state

States that fought with the North but later introduced legal segregation.

Bullwhipping

Beating a person with a heavy whip usually used to control cattle.

Take note

As you read this section, make notes linking the problems highlighted by the report and the recommendations for change. You could make a table.

Problems	Recommendations

and promote freedom across the world. However, he recognised that America could not fight for freedom abroad while segregation oppressed blacks in America's South. Truman was also motivated by the efforts of black campaigners. For example, A. Philip Randolph, encouraged blacks to refuse to join the American army because it remained segregated.

'To Secure These Rights' (1947)

In 1946, Truman established The President's Committee on Civil Rights. He commissioned them to produce a report examining the experience of racial minorities in America. The report, *To Secure These Rights*, highlighted the enormous problems facing African Americans, and proposed radical changes to make America a more just society.

The first problem highlighted was lynching. Between 1882 and 1945, there had been over 300 lynchings in five of the southern states.

Second, the report considered police brutality. The report frankly admitted that racist violence was widespread in the American police force. Indeed, it catalogued the methods used by white policemen against African Americans. These included barbaric practices such as pistol-whipping, beating prisoners with rubber hoses, dragging black prisoners through public areas, **bullwhipping**, the denial of medical treatment to black prisoners, and – in some cases – black prisoners being tied up and drowned. The report also argued that the police used many of these methods to force black prisoners to confess to crimes they had not committed.

Third, the report concerned voting rights. It noted that in the 1944 Presidential election, only 18 per cent of black people in the southern states had been able to vote due to legal obstacles such as grandfather clauses and literacy tests.

Fourth, *To Secure These Rights* described discrimination in the armed forces. Officially, the army, navy and air force claimed that there was no racial discrimination in their institutions. However, the report claimed that the experience of black people was wholly different. For example, in the army only one in 70 black soldiers was promoted to the rank of officer, whereas one in seven white soldiers received a promotion. Similarly, in the navy, there was one white officer for every seven white sailors, whereas of the 10,000 black sailors, only two had been promoted.

Fifth, the report considered employment and education. Black people clearly had fewer employment opportunities than whites. For example, 62 per cent of working black men were employed in the low-wage business of farming, compared with 28 per cent of working white men. Moreover, there was a significant wage gap between black and white workers. On average, black workers received 47 cents an hour, whereas white workers received 65 cents an hour. Similarly, black high school graduates earned on average $775 a year, while their white counterparts received $1,454 – almost double this amount. Discrimination was also evident in education. White teachers were paid considerably more than black teachers. For example, in Mississippi, the average annual salary of a white teacher was $1,107, whereas black teachers could expect to receive only $342.

Finally, the report detailed racial discrimination in the area of health. For example, in 1940 there was only one black doctor for every 3,377 black patients, while there was one white doctor for every 750 white patients. The report linked this to the refusal of many medical schools to accept black students.

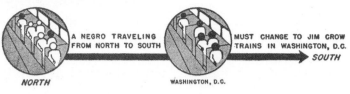

In summary, the report claimed that segregation was causing enormous problems for African Americans. Segregation was based on the idea that black and white facilities should be 'separate but equal'. However, the report showed that black people were not receiving equal treatment and segregation branded African Americans 'with the mark of inferiority and asserts [that they are] not fit to associate with white people.'

Diagram taken from *To Secure These Rights*, the report of the President's Committee on Civil Rights, published in 1947

Recommendations

The report recommended immediate and radical action to address the racial inequalities that bedevilled American society. The writers of the report explicitly linked this to the Cold War. They argued that 'the United States is not so strong, and the triumph of democracy is not so sure, that we can ignore what the world thinks of us or our record.'

To Secure These Rights argued that it was the job of federal government to protect and advance the civil rights of all Americans. In practice, this meant reorganising the Civil Rights Section of the Department of Justice so that regional offices could enforce civil rights at a local level. Additionally, the Civil Rights Section of the Department of Justice deserved greater government funding. The federal government could also promote civil rights by establishing permanent Presidential and Congressional committees to monitor racial equality and make proposals for its improvement. Finally, the report recommended that the federal government should not fund organisations that discriminate on the grounds of race.

New laws were proposed to deal with lynching, which would force the police to intervene to protect black citizens from mob violence, and allow the police to prosecute entire lynch mobs. Also, the report recommended new legislation to outlaw police brutality, and a Fair Employment Practices Act to end discrimination in employment and to make permanent the Fair Employment Practices Commission (FEPC) created by Roosevelt in 1941. At a local level, it was proposed that state governments should also establish committees to monitor and promote civil rights and state police forces should undergo compulsory training on race issues. State governments in the South should be forced to end segregation in education and healthcare, and all local initiatives which denied black citizens the right to vote should be abolished.

> **Source 3.2: From *To Secure These Rights***
>
> Democracy, brotherhood, human rights – these are practical expressions of the eternal worth of every child of God. With His guidance and help we can move forward toward a nobler social order in which there will be equal opportunity for all.

Glossary:

United Nations

An international organisation set up following the Second World War to provide a forum in which disagreements between nations could be resolved peacefully.

Dixiecrats

A slang term for southern Democrats who supported racial segregation.

The report accurately highlighted many of the problems facing African Americans. However, many of its recommendations were unworkable. For example, the report recommended that local police protect the black community and that local governments in the South should bring about desegregation. These suggestions were unrealistic for the simple reason that local police forces and local state governments were overwhelmingly racist and therefore had no intention of aiding black people. Nonetheless, in general terms the report suggested many essential reforms, such as the desegregation of the South.

Government action under Truman

Significantly, the report's proposals were only recommendations. In practice, Truman was not able to achieve everything that the report recommended, due to a lack of support in Congress.

Government appointments

Truman used his power as President to appoint African Americans to important government roles. Perhaps the most significant was Ralph Bunche, who was appointed American Ambassador to the **United Nations**. Working with the UN, Bunche mediated between Israelis and Palestinians, winning the Nobel Peace Prize for his work in 1950. In 1949, Truman appointed William Hastie as the first black federal judge.

The use of federal government power

In line with the recommendations of *To Secure These Rights*, Truman signed Executive Order 9980 guaranteeing fair employment practices in the civil service.

Truman also used government power to ensure that lucrative government defence contracts would not go to companies that discriminated against black people. To this end he signed Executive Order 10308 establishing the Committee on Government Contract Compliance (CGCC). Similarly, he prevented the Federal Housing Administration from lending money to building projects which would result in segregated housing. Finally, as part of his **'Fair Deal' programme** he committed the government to building houses in deprived urban areas in order to address some of the economic problems faced by African Americans.

Desegregation

Truman used his Presidential power to desegregate the American armed forces. This was an important symbolic step as the army was held in high esteem across the nation. In June 1948, Truman signed Executive Order 9981, guaranteeing 'equality of treatment and opportunity for all persons in the armed services without regard to race, colour, religion, or national origin.'

Truman's commitment to desegregation was also evident at his inauguration ceremony in 1949. Traditionally, the President had been inaugurated in front of a segregated crowd. Truman changed this, allowing black and white guests to sit alongside each other.

Truman also supported moves to desegregate Dulles Airport in Washington D.C. In 1950, these proposals were defeated, but Truman did manage to arrange the desegregation of the airport's restaurant. While this may appear a very small step towards racial equality, Truman saw it as highly significant: Dulles Airport was the first experience that many foreign dignitaries had of America and therefore Truman wanted it to reflect a truly democratic culture.

The 1948 Presidential election

The President of the United States is elected once every four years. Truman, who had been Vice-President under Roosevelt, became President on Roosevelt's death in 1945. The 1948 Presidential election was Truman's first attempt to be elected America's President. From the beginning of the campaign, Truman looked beaten: his commitment to civil rights had split his party. Democrats in the North praised Truman's anti-segregation policies. Southern Democrats, also known as **Dixiecrats**, refused to support Truman and put forward their own candidate for President – J. Strom Thurmond. The split in the Democratic Party seemed to assure a Republican victory in the election. It seemed to prove that an American President who was committed to black civil rights could never win an American election. Nonetheless, on Election Day, Truman won.

The 1948 Presidential election was ground-breaking because, for the first time, the American people elected a President who was committed to challenging segregation. Between 1945 and 1947, black Americans had not been convinced by Truman. Many believed that his fine words were not backed up by appropriate action. However, when Truman stood firm, rather than adopting racist policies to win over southern Dixiecrats, black voters began to believe that Truman meant what he said. Truman proved that it was possible to lose the votes of southern racists and still become President of the United States. Indeed, the black American vote for Truman proved to be significant in achieving his re-election.

How successful was Truman?

Truman was the first American President since Lincoln to publicly commit himself to a civil rights agenda. *To Secure These Rights* was a ground-breaking government report. It both detailed the scale of racial inequalities in America and mapped out a radical reform programme for addressing these inequalities. Truman's words were backed up by action. For example, Truman's decision to desegregate the armed forces and promote equality of employment in the civil service fulfilled some of the recommendations of the report and showed that he was committed to bringing about change.

However, Truman's achievements were limited. For example, the FEPC was under-funded and lacked support from senior civil servants. In addition, the Committee on Government Contract Compliance could not force defence companies to adopt fair employment practices. Truman's Fair Deal housing programme was poorly conceived. Under the programme, badly constructed

> **'Fair Deal' programme**
> US government initiative which aimed to tackle some economic inequalities, for example by providing public housing programmes and a higher minimum wage.

houses were demolished to make way for improved public housing. However, fewer houses were built than originally anticipated, and therefore the amount of housing available to African Americans actually decreased as a result of the programme. Finally, Truman's initiatives were simply not comprehensive enough to deal with the racism that existed at all levels of American society.

Taking it further

The whole text of *To Secure These Rights* is available online.

Throughout the report, diagrams have been used to illustrate the injustice faced by black Americans.

1. Which of the diagrams do you think most powerfully represents the racism of American society at the time?
2. What evidence can you find that other races also experienced discrimination in the USA?
3. Why do you think the authors of the report decided to include illustrations?

Activity: 'I'm Just Wild about Harry!'

Carry out *either one* of the following activities:

- It is 1948 and you have been employed as part of Truman's election campaign team. Your job is to encourage African Americans to vote for Truman. Design a campaign poster stressing Truman's civil rights record and his promises. Your poster will be more convincing if you include specific and accurate detail.

- It is 1948 and you are a member of a black civil rights pressure group. You are disappointed that Truman has not achieved more in terms of civil rights. Design a poster highlighting the limitations of Truman's achievements. Again, your poster will be more convincing if you include specific and accurate detail.

Chapter 4 Challenging 'Jim Crow'

Key questions

- What strategies were adopted by black people to challenge segregation in the USA?
- How effective were the NAACP's legal campaigns?
- Why was progress towards racial equality in America so slow in the period 1945–1955?

Alvin Jones is one of the forgotten heroes of the civil rights movement. Jones was a highly educated black man, who worked for the Louisiana Progressive Voters League. In June 1950, he spoke to a meeting of the Voters League in St Landry Parish, Louisiana. At the time, there was not a single black voter in the parish. Jones declared that this was unacceptable and the next day, he took five local black men to the Parish registrar. Before they could register to vote, Jones was assaulted by policemen armed with guns and knuckledusters. Although he survived this attack, he was beaten so badly that within 18 months he had died from his injuries. Civil rights campaigners took the police to court. However, all of the witnesses were either killed or fled before the case came to trial. The story of Alvin Jones illustrates the commitment of local campaigners to securing the rights of black people and the lengths to which white racists would go to stop them.

Timeline

1909	NAACP founded
1940–1957	CNO voter registration campaign in Arkansas
1944	*Smith v. Allwright*
1946	*Morgan v. Virginia*
1947	NAACP boycott of New Orleans department stores Journey of Reconciliation organised by CORE
1951	NAACP protest over school closures in Louisiana
1953	NAACP boycott a segregated school in Lafayette Baton Rouge bus boycott organised by UDL

Popular challenges to segregation

Protest groups worked tirelessly to overturn segregation, enfranchise black citizens and confront racism. The National Association for the Advancement of Colored People (NAACP) was one such group, best known for challenging segregation through the courts, although this was not their only tactic.

The decade after the Second World War has been described as the 'Golden Years of the NAACP.' During this period they operated a three-fold strategy to challenge segregation in the South. First, they took 'Jim Crow' laws to court. Second, they put pressure on politicians in Washington. Finally, they, along with other organisations, organised popular resistance to racism in the South.

Take note

Copy the timeline onto a large sheet of paper. As you work through this chapter, add details to the events mentioned. Make sure that when you are writing about a court case or an organised protest, you include information about its success or failure.

The NAACP and legal change

Who were the NAACP?

The NAACP was founded in 1909 by a multi-racial group of civil rights campaigners, headed by **W.E.B. DuBois**. It was created to fight for the rights of black people and to oppose discrimination and racial hatred. Between 1939 and 1942, the membership of the NAACP grew from 50,000 to 450,000. The NAACP is best known for its campaigning court cases which challenged the legal basis for segregation. Nonetheless, NAACP members were also involved with non-violent direct action and other initiatives to empower African Americans. For example, organisations such as the Louisiana Progressive Voters League, who aimed to encourage black voting registration, were subsections of the NAACP.

Why did the NAACP go to court?

The NAACP went to court because it believed that the American legal system could be used to end segregation. The American Constitution attempts to protect the rights of individuals through the separation of powers. That is to say, no one part of the American government is all-powerful. Consequently, American citizens can take federal and state government to court in cases where the government has acted in a way that appears to infringe their constitutional rights.

The strategy of the NAACP was to challenge 'Jim Crow' laws by appealing to the Fourteenth Amendment, which states that everyone born in the USA has full citizenship rights, and the Fifteenth Amendment, which states that all citizens have the right to vote, regardless of their colour.

In practice, the NAACP provided funds and experienced lawyers, such as **Thurgood Marshall**, in order to support the court cases of individual black men and women who were prepared to take the authorities to court. Two such cases were *Smith v. Allwright* (1944) and *Morgan v. Virginia* (1946).

Early court cases, 1944–1950

Smith v. Allwright, 1944

The case of *Smith v. Allwright* concerned the voting rights of black people in Texas. Although many black people in Texas could vote in Congressional elections they were excluded from **primary elections**. This was highly significant because Texas was a Democratic stronghold, so whoever won the Democratic primary would win the **Congressional election**. In this sense the primary election was more important than the Congressional election because the primary election effectively chose the winning candidate.

In 1944, Lonnie E. Smith, a black Texan, challenged this and with the backing of the NAACP he took his case all the way to the Supreme Court. White primaries were a feature of political life in many southern states including Virginia, Texas and Florida. The resulting court case ruled that the Texan white primary was illegal because all citizens, black or white, had the right to vote according to the Fifteenth Amendment. This was extremely important because the Supreme Court's rulings applied to the whole of America. Consequently, *Smith v. Allwright* outlawed all-white primaries throughout America.

Morgan v. Virginia, 1946

Morgan v. Virginia challenged segregation on interstate bus services (bus services that run between different states). In 1944, Irene Morgan was fined $100 for refusing to give up her seat on an interstate bus to a white man. Morgan argued that segregation on interstate transport violated her constitutional rights. Consequently, she took her case, again with the backing of the NAACP's chief lawyer Thurgood Marshall, to the Supreme Court. In 1946, the Supreme Court ruled that segregation on interstate buses was illegal.

Non-violent resistance, 1945–1955

Legal action is only one part of the story of the early struggle for civil rights. Indeed, it was in the years 1945–1955 that African Americans developed the tactics of **direct action** that they would use so successfully in the late 1950s and early 1960s.

Between 1945 and 1955, the NAACP organised a series of protests in the southern state of Louisiana. For example, in 1947 the NAACP and its supporters **picketed** New Orleans' four biggest department stores for refusing to allow black customers to try on hats. In 1951, the NAACP tried the same tactic in the town of Alexandra in protest at the fact that the local black school would close during the cotton harvest so that black children could work in the fields. In 1953 the NAACP organised a **boycott** of a newly built school in Lafayette, protesting that its facilities were obviously inferior to those enjoyed at the local white school.

The NAACP was not the only group involved in direct action in the forties and fifties; other groups such as United Defence League (UDL), the Committee on Negro Organization (CNO), the Congress of Industrial Organizations (CIO) and the Congress of Racial Equality (CORE) were also active during this period.

The UDL organised a week-long bus boycott in Louisiana's capital Baton Rouge in June 1953. The boycott was accompanied by 'Operation Free Lift', a car pooling scheme which transported African Americans around the city in over 100 private cars. Additionally, between 1940 and 1957, the CNO organised a voter registration campaign in the southern state of Arkansas.

CORE's Journey of Reconciliation (1947)

The Supreme Court's decision in the case of *Morgan v. Virginia* (1946) meant that segregating interstate transport was now illegal. However, this **de jure** change did not lead to the **de facto** desegregation that the campaigners sought. As a result, in 1947 a team of 16 CORE activists (eight black and eight white) planned to travel by bus from the northern states to the southern states. Their objective was to draw public attention to the fact that many bus companies in the South were ignoring the *Morgan v. Virginia* ruling.

The Journey of Reconciliation started on 9 April 1947 and lasted for two weeks. Black team members sat in the white areas of the bus, and white team members sat in those areas designated for blacks. The campaign

Glossary:

Direct action

A form of protest that involves large groups of people and draws public attention to injustice.

Picket

A form of protest in which people block access to a building that represents the cause which they are protesting against.

Boycott

Refusing to buy goods or services.

De jure* and *de facto

De jure refers to something defined or stated in law. *De facto* refers to how something happens in practice. Notably, a change in the law does not necessarily lead to an immediate change in practice.

successfully proved that bus companies in the southern states were ignoring the Supreme Court's ruling.

Overall, the Journey of Reconciliation resulted in the arrests of 12 CORE members. However, it failed to force southern states such as North Carolina to desegregate its interstate bus services.

How successful was direct action between 1945 and 1955?

The direct action campaigns in the decade after the Second World War had mixed results. CNO's Arkansas-based voter registration campaign, for example, increased the proportion of black voters in the state from 1.5 per cent of the black population in 1940 to 17.3 per cent in 1947. Other successful initiatives included the NAACP's lynching investigation squad. In 1946 the NAACP set up a special unit of lawyers and investigators who would visit lynching scenes, collect evidence and mount court cases to bring the perpetrators to justice. This was very successful and was part of the reason that lynching, which had been commonplace in 1940, was on the decline by 1955.

On the other hand, CORE's Journey of Reconciliation failed to force bus companies in southern states to desegregate their interstate services. Similarly, the UDL's bus boycott was unsuccessful, and Baton Rouge's buses remained segregated. Nonetheless, even the failures had positive consequences. The UDL's action failed because the boycott was too short to attract media attention or to hurt the bus company's finances. But later campaigns would learn from the UDL's experience and organise more effectively as a result. Also, the boycott involved the black community of an entire city in protest. Equally, CORE's Journey of Reconciliation was groundbreaking because it linked a legal campaign with non-violent protest. This experience of protest, like the NAACP's campaigns across the South, increased the confidence of African Americans and showed that it was possible to stand up to segregation.

Activity: Reasons for change

In the last two chapters you have studied three different factors that led to increased rights for black Americans by 1953: Presidential action, court cases, and direct action.

Using the information in Chapters 3 and 4, complete the following table, assessing the impact of each factor on the struggle for equal rights. Write a paragraph explaining which factor you consider to have been most important. Support your opinion with detailed examples.

Factor	Examples	Achievements	Limitations
Presidential action			
Court cases			
Direct action			

Chapter 5   Raising the profile of civil rights – kicking 'Jim Crow' out of school

---

Key questions

- Why did the NAACP target education?
- Why was *Brown II* necessary?
- What was the reaction to the NAACP's legal victories?

In a modern society it should be easy for children to attend their local school. However, this was not the case for seven-year-old Linda Brown. Linda's fight to attend her local school went all the way to the Supreme Court. What is more, it led to a constitutional crisis that some felt might cause a new American civil war.

Timeline

1950	*Sweatt v. Painter*
1954	*Brown v. Board of Education of Topeka* White Citizens' Councils formed
1955	*Brown v. Board of Education* (II) Emmett Till lynched
1956	Southern Manifesto signed NAACP banned from Alabama

The NAACP and education

The National Association for the Advancement of Colored People (NAACP) targeted education because it was easy to show that while children were being educated separately, they were not being educated equally. In this sense, the NAACP could highlight the fact that segregated education was illegal in terms of the *Plessy v. Ferguson* ruling of 1896 (see pages 9–10). The inequalities in education were staggering. For example, in 1949, the state of South Carolina spent an average of $179 a year educating a white child, whereas black children were educated for an average of $43 a year.

A second reason for challenging racism in education was the belief that

> ### Take note
>
> As you work through this chapter, try the following method of note-taking:
> 1. Divide your paper into two columns, with the left-hand column only a third the width of the right-hand column.
> 2. In the left-hand column, write only the section headings and the points that you think are most important. Try and write as little as possible in this column.
> 3. In the right-hand column, make detailed notes with specific examples.

Source 5.1: Civil rights campaigner Ralph Thompson recalls his education in the segregated South

We did reading and writing, but we didn't go beyond that. And I guess that was part of segregation. And, to see other white kids that could play baseball and things like that we were denied. That was a little hard for us back then.

Taken from: *Remembering Jim Crow*, eds. Chafe, Gavins and Korstadt (2001)

Segregated school in the backwoods of Georgia, 1941. Black children studied in deprived conditions and there was only one teacher.

improving the education of African Americans was a vital first step towards improving the lives of African Americans more generally. Indeed, a good education was seen as a prerequisite to getting a good job and a secure income.

Sweatt v. Painter (1950)

The NAACP's first successful challenge to segregation in education was the 1950 case of *Sweatt v. Painter*. Heman Sweatt was a black student hoping to study law in the southern state of Texas. However, the Texan education system was segregated, and therefore Sweatt was refused admission to the University of Texas Law School. The NAACP challenged this, arguing that Sweatt was entitled to an education equal to that of whites at the Law School. The courts in Texas decided that the state had no duty to integrate the Law School. Rather, they ordered the creation of a law school specifically for black students. The NAACP rejected this ruling and took the case to the Supreme Court. They argued that the new law school was inferior to the white school of law. As an example of this, they demonstrated that the black school had fewer students, fewer teachers and fewer books. The Supreme Court agreed with the NAACP and ordered the University of Texas Law School to accept Sweatt as a student. Sweatt registered as a student at the law school on 19 September 1950.

Brown v. Board of Education of Topeka (1954)

The NAACP's success in the case of *Sweatt v. Painter* concerned the rights of students to graduate-level education. The Brown case of 1954 dealt with the rights of younger students. Oliver Brown took the state of Kansas to court for failing to provide adequate education for his daughter. Linda Brown was forced to attend an all-black school that was 20 blocks away from her home. Her father argued that she would be better served attending the local white school, which was much closer to their house. Again, the NAACP took the case all the way to the Supreme Court. After three years of legal battles, the Supreme Court unanimously decided that segregation was illegal in American schools. The Supreme Court's decision was a turning point in the civil rights struggle. Essentially, the Court argued that 'separate but equal' – established in the case of *Plessy v. Ferguson* – was a contradiction in terms. That is to say, they believed that it was impossible for citizens to receive services that were both 'separate' and 'equal'. In this way, the Brown case was significant because it marked an end to the doctrine of 'separate but equal'.

The Supreme Court's decision

The Supreme Court made its decision for five main reasons.

- First, they argued that segregation had a negative effect on black children.

- Second, the Supreme Court recognised that America was changing. Between 1945 and 1954, there had been a considerable growth in the black middle class, due in part to the migration in the earlier part of the century. Middle-class African Americans were more assertive and had a better understanding of America's legal system, and were therefore more likely to challenge racial inequality in the courts. Consequently, the Supreme Court felt under greater pressure to rule in their favour.
- Third, the Supreme Court believed that for over 60 years southern states failed to provide education that was genuinely equal. Indeed, the Court recognised that southern states lacked the economic resources to raise the standards of black schools. Consequently, the only way to ensure equal provision in education was to integrate the school system.
- Fourth, the Supreme Court recognised that a racist education system did not reflect the ideals that America was fighting for in the Cold War. America claimed to be fighting for freedom and justice against the communist dictatorships that dominated Russia and Eastern Europe. At least one Supreme Court judge stated that segregated education undermined America's ability to champion democracy.
- Finally, the decision was reached because of a change in the leadership of the Supreme Court. Chief Judge Frederick Moore Vinson died in 1953 and was replaced by **Earl Warren**. Warren was much more sympathetic to civil rights issues and used his authority to persuade the other members of the Supreme Court that segregation in education could no longer be tolerated.

Immediate reaction to the Brown case

Black American reaction

Many African Americans believed that the Brown case was the beginning of the end of segregation. For this reason, black campaigners believed that the Supreme Court would back legal challenges to segregation in other areas of American life. Following this case, there was an increase in local activism by groups such as the NAACP and CORE, who organised new voter registration campaigns and local protests against different aspects of segregation.

White backlash

Southern racists also saw the significance of the Brown case. Consequently, the NAACP's success provoked a series of initiatives across the South which aimed to undermine the ruling. First, middle-class whites set up White Citizens' Councils to demand that segregation continued in local schools. The White Citizens' Councils also raised money to help support white state schools that decided to become private in order to avoid desegregating. Additionally, the Councils campaigned for the election of local politicians who were strongly opposed to desegregation. By 1956, 250,000 people had joined White Citizens' Councils.

Second, there was a revival in the activity of the Ku Klux Klan. Indeed, less than a year after the Brown Case, **Emmett Till**, a 14-year-old black boy, was lynched, and his murderers were found not guilty by an all-white jury in spite of intensive campaigns by the NAACP.

Earl Warren

(1891–1974)

A Republican judge and Supreme Court Justice. As Chief Justice (the head of the Supreme Court) he was involved in a series of landmark cases that destroyed the legal basis of segregation.

Emmett Till

(1941–1955)

Emmett Till was raised in the northern city of Chicago, Illinois. During a visit to his Uncle in Money, Mississippi, he was accused of flirting with a white woman and was subsequently lynched by her relatives. Till's mother insisted that his coffin was left open at his funeral. She said 'I wanted the world to see what they did to my baby', a reference to the fact that his face had been appallingly disfigured in a horrific beating.

Protestors at a pro-segregation rally in Baltimore, 1954

Third, there was a sustained attack on the NAACP. For example, Alabama's state court officially outlawed the NAACP and banned all of its activities. Similarly, in Louisiana, police persecution of the NAACP led to the closure of 48 of its 50 branches.

Fourth, Senator Harry F. Byrd called on white southerners to put up 'massive resistance', meaning that the white people of the South should defend segregation with all their strength. In 1956, Byrd led 101 southern Congressmen who signed the 'Southern Manifesto'. The Manifesto argued that the Supreme Court's decision in the Brown case was unconstitutional because the constitution did not even mention education. It also asserted that southern states should continue to implement segregation in accordance with the doctrine of 'separate but equal'. Lastly, the Manifesto called on all Americans to resist desegregation 'by all lawful means.'

The President

President Dwight D. Eisenhower, who had succeeded Truman in 1953, refused to comment on the Brown decision. In private, he criticised the ruling, arguing that a legal change would do nothing to change the hearts and minds of southern white racists. In essence, Eisenhower believed that *de jure* change was incapable of producing *de facto* change. Moreover, Eisenhower believed that the Brown ruling was counter-productive. Rather than producing a desegregated education system, all Brown had done was to infuriate white citizens and whip up tremendous opposition to black civil rights. Finally, in private Eisenhower claimed that his decision to make Earl Warren Chief Justice was 'the biggest damned-fool mistake I ever made.'

Brown II (1955)

The Brown case was highly significant, but in the first year the *de jure* victory resulted in little *de facto* change. Consequently, the NAACP asked the Supreme Court to establish a timetable for desegregating southern schools. In response, the Supreme Court produced the *Brown II* ruling, stating that the desegregation of education should occur 'with all deliberate speed'. The decision pleased no one. The NAACP believed that the ruling was too vague to force any change. Southern racists, on the other hand, saw this as a further attack on segregation.

The significance of the Brown case

The Brown case was highly symbolic. For the first time, the NAACP had won a case that struck at the heart of segregation. Additionally, the Supreme Court under Chief Justice Earl Warren had clearly signalled that it was sympathetic to the civil rights cause.

In spite of this, the Brown case failed to bring about the wholesale desegregation of the southern education system. For example, by 1957, only 750 of 6,300 southern school districts had desegregated. Consequently, only 3 per cent of black students in the South were educated in mixed schools. Indeed, as late as 1968, 58 per cent of southern black school children remained in segregated schools. Clearly, the Brown case showed that *de jure* change was of little use without a clear time frame.

The Brown case was also significant because it stimulated 'massive resistance'. The Ku Klux Klan, White Citizens' Councils, southern white politicians, white policemen, and judges in local courts united to oppose desegregation. Additionally, the Brown case demonstrated that Eisenhower was unwilling to use his presidential power to help black people. Indeed, his refusal even to welcome the decision showed that he had no intention of getting involved in civil rights issues.

Conclusion

In the period 1945 to 1955 campaigning methods changed and developed in several ways. Initially, campaigners had most success with court cases such as *Morgan v. Virginia*, *Sweatt v. Painter* and *Brown v. Board of Education*, which showed that segregation was unconstitutional. However, these *de jure* victories were slow to produce *de facto* desegregation. As a result, groups such as CORE and the NAACP organised popular campaigns to test the implementation of Supreme Court rulings and challenge segregation at a grassroots level. Finally, the Brown case highlighted the reluctance of white authorities to put Supreme Court rulings into action. Therefore, the NAACP demanded a time frame to force the southern authorities to comply.

Despite the efforts of groups such as the NAACP and CORE, progress towards desegregation was slow. Indeed, there were five main reasons for the continuation of segregation in the first decade after the Second World War.

- Many within the US Congress were opposed to racial integration. Indeed, almost a fifth of Congressmen signed the racist Southern Manifesto of 1956. What is more, even those who were not openly racist were reluctant to support Truman's civil rights reforms (see Chapter 3, page 20).
- President Eisenhower believed that desegregation could not be forced upon the South. He thought that change would happen over time, but that it was not the President's job to dictate change.
- Southern state governments, southern judges and the southern police resisted change and used their power to intimidate campaigners fighting for an end to segregation.
- Southern white racists organised quickly and effectively to ensure that court rulings were ignored.
- Finally, civil rights organisations such as CORE and the NAACP had not yet perfected their methods. Nonetheless, this would soon change and the late 1950s saw a new dawn for the black civil rights movement.

Activity: Plotting progress

1. Draw the following graph, with the *y*-axis labelled 'Effect on conditions for black Americans', and the *x*-axis with the dates from 1950–1956.

2. Look at the timeline on page 27. Plot the events onto the graph, showing when they happened and the extent to which they improved conditions for African Americans. Draw a line to link the points.

4. Write a paragraph in answer to the question: 'How far did conditions for black Americans improve in the period 1950–1956?' Do not describe the shape of the graph. Instead, use it to reach an overall judgement then support this judgement with specific examples.

Activity: This house believes...

Taking it further

The impact of segregation on American schoolchildren should not be underestimated. Research Jane Elliott's 1968 'Blue Eyes, Brown Eyes' experiment then answer the following questions:

1. What exactly did Jane Elliott do as part of her experiment?
2. In what ways did she seek to replicate segregation in education?
3. What were the results of her experiment?

Students should be organised into two teams. The first team must defend the motion: 'This house believes that by 1955, significant progress had been made towards racial equality for black Americans.' The second team must oppose it.

Spend some time preparing for this debate. Use the information in Chapters 1–5 to find general points and specific examples to support your argument. Remember, this question is about the extent to which equality had been achieved, not the methods used to fight for equality.

● Each team should appoint a team leader. With the help of the team, the team leader should prepare a five-minute speech outlining the team's argument.

● An impartial Chair should also be appointed, to oversee the debate, ensure politeness and award points.

The structure of the debate

1. Seat the two teams facing each other, with the team leaders in central positions.
2. The Chair should introduce the debate and welcome the teams. The Chair should then invite the team leaders to present their speeches, proposing and opposing the motion.
3. Following the speeches, the floor is opened for contributions (in the form of questions or comments) from the other members of the team. Points are awarded by the Chair as follows: relevant question 1 point; general statement 2 points; statement supported by a specific example 3 points.
4. At the end of the debate, the team with the most points is declared the winner.

Skills Builder 1: **Writing in paragraphs**

What should you include in a paragraph?

In a paragraph you should:

- make a point to support your argument and answer the question

- provide evidence to support your point

- explain how your evidence supports your point

- explain how your point relates to the essay question.

Remember: POINT – EVIDENCE – EXPLANATION

It is important that you construct your answer this way. If you just 'tell a story' in which you produce factual knowledge without explanation, you will not get high marks.

An example

Here is an example of a question asking you to produce not a story, but an explanation:

> (A) Why was progress towards racial equality so slow in the period 1945–1955?

The information to answer this question can be found in Section 1. The reasons you could include are:

- political factors – opposition from senior politicians

- popular opposition – racism among the general public

- ineffective methods of protest – campaigns are not co-ordinated to create maximum impact

- legal factors – segregation has a legal basis, and legal methods of campaigning are slow

- widespread nature of discrimination – racism affects all aspects of life for black Americans, and is therefore difficult to counter.

As you plan, it is important to have a clear idea about the relative importance of the factors you are discussing. You should decide which factor is most important.

Your answer should be clearly written and you should aim to convince the examiner that your opinion is correct.

Here is an example of a paragraph that could form part of your answer:

The most important reason why progress towards racial equality was so slow in the period 1945–1955 was the opposition of white politicians. For example, Senators blocked Truman's attempt to make the FEPC permanent. Indeed, Truman was unwilling to implement the full recommendations of the 1947 report *To Secure These Rights*. This was because southern Democrats, or Dixiecrats as they were known, had powerful positions within Congress and would use these to block his other initiatives if he had attempted to push through widespread desegregation. Clearly, this opposition was the most important reason; without it, Truman would have had much greater scope to pursue the changes recommended in *To Secure These Rights*.

This is a good paragraph because:

- It begins with a clear point that directly answers the question.

- It prioritises, showing which point was the most important.

- The opening statement is backed up by evidence. The paragraph contains detailed examples about the opposition of white politicians.

- The final sentences clearly link the opposition with the lack of progress.

Activity: Spot the mistake

Below are three paragraphs which attempt to explain why political factors were the most important obstacle to progress in the period 1945–1955. However, although the information in each paragraph is correct, there are mistakes in the way each paragraph is written. Your task is to spot the mistake and write one sentence of advice to the author of each paragraph explaining how they could do better.

Example 1:

The most important reason why progress towards racial equality was so slow in this period was the opposition of powerful politicians. For example, prior to Abraham Lincoln, American Presidents had not opposed slavery. Even after Lincoln, American politicians did nothing while the southern states imposed 'Jim Crow' laws. Later, President Roosevelt showed that he opposed even basic civil rights for black Americans when he refused to back an anti-lynching bill. Therefore, progress towards racial equality was slow in this period because the Presidents did little to protect the rights of black Americans.

Example 2:

In 1945, Harry S. Truman became President. He commissioned a report entitled 'To Secure These Rights'. This report showed that there was widespread discrimination towards black Americans. Truman also desegregated the armed forces and Washington airport's canteen. But Truman didn't care about the rights of black people. Instead, he cared about gaining votes for himself. He thought that if he appeared to care about civil rights, more black people would vote for him.

Example 3:

Between 1945 and 1955 progress towards racial equality was slow for a number of reasons. However, there was some progress. For example, in 1954, the NAACP fought a case known as the Brown Case. The Supreme Court ruled that Linda Brown should be allowed to attend a white school that was nearer to her home than the school for black children. In effect, this ended segregation in education. Brown II in 1955 went further, stating that schools should desegregate 'with all deliberate speed'. These were not the first successful court cases. In 1950, the case Sweatt v. Painter had ended all-white primary elections, giving black Americans greater political rights. In this way, although full equality was not achieved in this period, there was some progress in the areas of education and political rights.

Answers:

Example 1 – the information is outside the period specified in the question and therefore cannot be credited by the examiner.

Example 2 – the information is within the period specified, but does not explicitly answer the question. Instead, it 'tells the story'.

Example 3 – the answer addresses the wrong question, focusing on progress rather than reasons for limited progress.

Chapter 6   Civil rights protests: the early southern campaigns, 1955–1962

Key questions

- How did the campaign methods used by the civil rights protestors develop in the period 1955–1962?
- What was achieved by the key protests of this period?
- Why were these protests significant?

The groups that we call 'the civil rights movement' rarely used that term. They simply called themselves 'the movement'. This indicated that the goals of the movement were much bigger than 'civil rights'. Martin Luther King wanted not just the death of legal segregation; he wanted the birth of a 'beloved community' in which black and white people were an integral part of one another's lives. The term implied a journey and a direction and unstoppable momentum.

Introduction

From 1955 to 1962 the civil rights movement organised a series of campaigns addressing transport, education and the segregation of public places.

Montgomery bus boycott (1955–1956)

Segregation in Alabama

Buses throughout the South were segregated. Normally, this meant that the front rows of the bus were reserved for white people while black people were forced to sit at the back. Additionally, if the bus was full, black people had to give up their seats to white people.

In 1955 **Claudette Colvin** demonstrated that there was widespread support in Montgomery for challenging bus segregation. The National Association for the Advancement of Colored People (NAACP) turned to **Rosa Parks**, a long-standing member in order to challenge segregation.

On 1 December 1955, Parks refused to leave her seat and allow a white man to take her place. As a result she was arrested and fined $14. Parks' arrest led to a two-pronged attack on segregation laws in Alabama. First, the NAACP mounted a legal case to challenge the segregation laws. Second, the black people of Montgomery began a campaign of **direct action** targeting local bus companies.

MIA and the boycott

Following Parks' arrest local NAACP leader **E.D. Nixon** was quick to call a meeting of Montgomery's black leaders in order to oppose segregation. As a result the Montgomery Improvement Association (MIA) was established under the leadership of Martin Luther King in order to co-ordinate a boycott

Take note

As you read through this chapter, make a timeline of important events. Add details to the events mentioned on your timeline. You may wish to record:

- the aims of the protests
- the methods used
- the civil rights groups involved
- the achievements of the protests.

Then use your notes to answer the following questions:

1. How far did the aims of the civil rights protestors change during this period?
2. How far did the methods of the civil rights protestors change during this period?

Claudette Colvin

(born 1939)

Nine months before the Montgomery bus boycott, Colvin, then aged 15, refused to give up her bus seat to a white passenger. The NAACP considered using her case to protest the segregation of transport. However, in the months following her arrest, Colvin, who was not married, became pregnant. Consequently, it was felt that she was not an appropriate figurehead for the protest.

Rosa Parks

(1913–2005)

Parks joined the Montgomery branch of the NAACP in 1943. She was also part of the Women's Political Council which mobilised women and played a key role in the success of the boycott. Following the Montgomery bus boycott, she became a prominent figure in the civil rights movement. She died in 2005, and as a mark of respect she was given a state funeral and all American flags were flown at half-mast.

E.D. Nixon

(1899–1987)

A long-standing civil rights activist and union organiser based in Montgomery, Alabama.

Mohandas Gandhi

(1869–1948)

The leader of India's independence movement. Gandhi fought British colonial rule using non-violent tactics.

of the local buses until segregation was abolished. The MIA worked mainly through black churches. Its Christian basis meant that it was committed to non-violent methods.

King's philosophy

King preached a distinctive philosophy based on the teachings of Jesus and the example of **Mohandas Gandhi**. King was a well educated middle-class Christian. He believed that Christians should love their enemies and never retaliate. Nonetheless, he also taught that Christians should stand up to injustice. Consequently, he advocated **civil disobedience** and direct action, insisting that protest should always be peaceful.

The progress of the boycott

Nixon's swift action meant that the boycott began on the day after Parks was fined. The campaign lasted for over a year, during which time over 85 per cent of Montgomery's black community boycotted the buses. In order to sustain the boycott the MIA organised initiatives such as **car pooling**.

The boycott hit the bus companies hard. The majority of the company's passengers were black and consequently they lost 65 per cent of their revenue. The Montgomery authorities soon realised the significance of the boycott, and following a march they arrested King along with 156 other prominent black protestors. King was fined $500 and sentenced to a year in prison. However, the arrest backfired and drew media attention to the campaign. King proclaimed that he was proud of his crime and served just two weeks of his sentence.

Browder v. Gayle (1956)

The Montgomery bus boycott itself did not change the segregation laws. Rather, the NAACP's court case *Browder v. Gayle* ended in a US Supreme Court ruling that made the segregation of buses illegal. The case started in April 1955 when Aurelia Browder was arrested for refusing to give up her bus seat to a white person. Browder appealed against her conviction and with the support of the NAACP the case went all the way to the Supreme Court. On 20 December 1956 the court outlawed segregation of buses.

Desegregation on the buses

On 21 December 1956 the Montgomery Bus Company desegregated their buses, allowing black passengers to sit wherever they liked. The Montgomery campaign was highly significant in the following ways:
- It showed the economic power of black citizens – the boycott had financially crippled the bus companies thereby highlighting the importance of black customers.

- It demonstrated the power of uniting popular direct action with an NAACP legal campaign.
- It highlighted the significance of media involvement – television reports had portrayed the injustice of segregation to a national and international audience.
- It demonstrated Martin Luther King's leadership qualities and brought him to national attention.
- It showed the lengths to which the white authorities would go to defend segregation.
- It indicated that the Supreme Court was willing to overturn *Plessy v. Ferguson* (see pages 9–10).
- The success of the Montgomery bus boycott led to the establishment of the **Southern Christian Leadership Conference (SCLC)**. King hoped that the SCLC would keep the spirit of the Montgomery protest alive.

The Little Rock Campaign (1957)

By 1957, the *de facto* desegregation of education in the southern states had made little progress (see Chapter 5, page 31). The 1957 Little Rock Campaign attempted to speed up school desegregation by enrolling nine black students into Little Rock's all-white Central High School. Local Governor Orval Faubus opposed the enrolment and ordered the **National Guard** to prevent the nine black students entering the school. Consequently, on 3 September 1957 the National Guard, backed by a white mob, refused to let the students into the school.

President Eisenhower ordered Governor Faubus to withdraw the National Guard. At the same time the **US Department of Justice** gained a **court injunction** forcing the governor to withdraw the National Guard. Faubus complied, but the students were still prevented from enrolling due to the presence of crowds of white racists. The unrest prompted Eisenhower to take the National Guard under Presidential control, ordering them to protect the black students. As a result, on 25 September the students, escorted by the National Guard, enrolled at Little Rock Central High School.

Faubus, however, did not admit defeat. Backed by racists in the Arkansas legislature he passed a law giving him the power to close local schools in order to avoid desegregation. Faubus used this power to close the schools in Little Rock. As a result 4000 students, black and white, were forced to seek education elsewhere. Again, the NAACP went to court, in *Cooper v. Aaron* (1958). As a result the Supreme Court ruled that it was illegal to prevent desegregation for any reason. Consequently, in June 1959 the schools in Little Rock re-opened and had to accept black and white students.

The significance of Little Rock

The NAACP's campaign at Little Rock was significant in the following ways:
- It demonstrated the effectiveness of testing Supreme Court Rulings – ensuring that *de jure* change led to *de facto* change (see page 25).
- The campaign forced Eisenhower to intervene to support desegregation – in this way the campaign gained the authority of the US President.

Glossary:

Civil disobedience

The active refusal to obey unjust laws.

Car pooling

The practice of sharing cars.

Direct action

A form of political action which does not use standard political institutions such as elections, courts of law or political parties. Rather, it uses popular campaigns such as marches, boycotts or sit-ins.

National Guard

A military force made up of reservists, people who are called upon in emergencies rather than being professional soldiers. The National Guard is usually controlled by state governors. However, it can be 'federalised' and brought under the control of the President.

US Department of Justice

The Federal Government's department for dealing with law and order.

Court injunction

A court order insisting that a group or individual refrains from certain actions.

> The opposition of the State Governor, the Arkansas legislature and the protestors showed the extent to which white Southerners opposed integration.

Greensboro sit-ins (1960)

The Greensboro sit-ins shifted the focus of the civil rights movement towards public places such as restaurants, swimming pools and libraries.

In February 1960 four local students entered a Woolworth's store in Greensboro, North Carolina (see map on page 39), and sat on 'whites-only' seats at the counter, refusing to leave until they were served. The protest escalated; 27 students came on the second day; 300 by the fourth. By the end of the week the store closed temporarily in order to halt the sit-ins.

The sit-ins were hugely influential. Within a week similar protests had occurred in six towns in North Carolina, and within a month sit-ins were taking place in six more states. Activists staged 'wade-ins' at segregated swimming pools, 'read-ins' in segregated libraries, 'watch-ins' in cinemas and 'kneel-ins' at white-only churches. By the beginning of 1961 over 70,000 people, black and white, had taken part in demonstrations against the segregation of public places.

Four African American college students' sit-in protest at a whites-only lunch counter at a Woolworth's store during the second day of the Greensboro sit-ins, February 1960.

> ## The SCLC
>
> The SCLC was designed to help organise protests across America. However, it was not intended as a rival to the NAACP. Indeed, it refused to take individual members as this would have been in direct competition with the NAACP. The SCLC was committed to nonviolent protest, adopting the motto 'not one hair, of one head, of one person should be harmed'.

SNCC and the significance of the sit-ins

As the sit-in movement spread, King's SCLC became involved in organising and co-ordinating action. At the same time, a new civil rights organisation was formed: the **Student Nonviolent Coordinating Committee (SNCC)**.

The sit-ins of 1960 and 1961 were significant for the following reasons:

- They increased the number of civil rights organisations and showed they could co-operate effectively.
- They demonstrated that civil rights campaigns could spread quickly and affect the whole of the South.
- Media coverage allowed the whole of America to witness the level of persecution faced by the protestors. This brought increased support for the civil rights movement.
- The sit-ins attacked all aspects of segregation in the South, extending the existing NAACP campaigns against segregation in education.
- The sit-ins showed the economic power of black people in the South – Woolworth's profits decreased by a third during the campaign.
- By the end of 1961, 810 towns had desegregated their public places. Six months after the campaign started, black people were finally served at the lunch counter of the Greensboro Woolworth's store.

'You don't have to ride Jim Crow' – the Freedom Rides (1961)

The Freedom Rides were designed to turn the *de jure* victories of *Morgan v.*

Virginia and **Boynton v. Virginia** into *de facto* desegregation of interstate transport and interstate transport facilities. The Freedom Riders sought to test these rulings by travelling from Washington DC to New Orleans on interstate transport.

The Freedom Rides campaign was organised by the Congress of Racial Equality (CORE). A group of seven black and six white activists from CORE and SNCC set out on Greyhound and Trailways buses on 4 May 1961.

The Freedom Riders expected to meet violent opposition and planned to use this to gain media attention. In Anniston, local police officers, working hand-in-hand with the Ku Klux Klan, refused to intervene when a white mob fire-bombed the Freedom Riders' bus. Similarly, in Birmingham, the Police Chief Eugene 'Bull' Connor refused to protect the Freedom Riders. He even granted most of the local police the day off, giving a green light to local racists. In Montgomery, too, the police and medics refused to intervene even after a white crowd beat the Riders with baseball bats. Following this outrage, King, who had previously refused to be involved, gave a speech at a rally in support of the Freedom Riders.

The Freedom Riders achieved a significant victory by forcing Attorney General **Robert Kennedy** to enforce desegregation of the interstate bus services.

The significance of the Freedom Rides

The Freedom Rides were significant in the following ways:

- They marked a new high point of co-operation within the civil rights movement as they involved CORE, SNCC and the SCLC.
- They showed that the new Kennedy administration was sympathetic towards civil rights.

The Albany Movement (1961–1962)

Following the Freedom Rides, the SNCC targeted Albany, Georgia, and organised protests to end segregation. Local Police Chief Laurie Pritchett had studied the strategy of the protestors and adopted a new approach designed to deny them media attention. For example, he ordered the local police to treat protestors with respect in public and to prevent racist violence. Furthermore, King was arrested during the campaign and there is evidence that Pritchett arranged to have him released in order to prevent his incarceration gaining publicity. Finally, Pritchett made general promises that conditions would improve which led to little concrete action.

SNCC

The SNCC was created in April 1960 with the intention of helping to organise the demonstrations. The SNCC, like the NAACP, accepted members and indeed, they attracted black and white activists. Like the SCLC, SNCC was committed to nonviolent forms of struggle.

Boynton v. Virginia

A court case in 1960 which established that the segregation of interstate bus services was illegal.

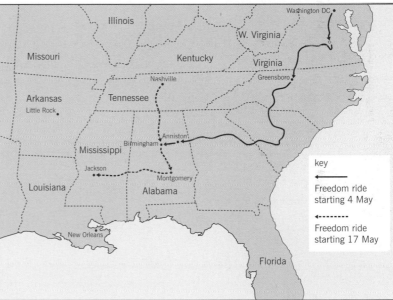

Route of Freedom Rides starting 4 May and 17 May 1961. The planned destination for the first freedom ride was New Orleans, but it was forced to end in Birmingham following mob violence. A second ride followed on 17 May, starting in Nashville; the ride was forced to end in Jackson, where demonstrators were jailed.

Robert Kennedy

(1925–1968)

Brother of President John F. Kennedy. He served his brother as Attorney General – the head of the Justice Department. He ran for President in 1968, but was assassinated during the campaign.

Taking it further

In 1959, a white American journalist, John Howard Griffin, endured medical treatments to change his skin colour and spent a month living as a black American in the South. He said, 'Black men told me that the only way a white man could hope to understand anything about racism was to wake up some morning in a black man's skin.' His account of this period was published in the book *Black Like Me*. Find a copy of this book. How useful is his account to an historian studying race relations in the USA?

The significance of the Albany Movement

The Albany Movement was significant in the following ways:

- It showed that peaceful protest did not always bring about change.
- It led to divisions within the civil rights movement. Radicals in SNCC began to talk about using violence to challenge segregation as peaceful protest was proving less effective.
- King acknowledged that his tactics had not worked and stated that future campaigns needed to be more focused on a specific issue and target police chiefs who were more likely to respond with violence.

James Meredith and the University of Mississippi (1962)

James Meredith's personal campaign took the civil rights struggle back to education. In 1962 Meredith attempted to become the first black student at the University of Mississippi. Ross Barnett, the Governor of Mississippi, refused to allow Meredith to enrol. The Supreme Court, however, backed Meredith, and President Kennedy put pressure on Barnett to back down and ensure that Meredith was able to take his place at the University. However, Barnett refused to provide Meredith with protection and, as a result, when he arrived on campus he faced a mob of violent white protestors who prevented him from enrolling.

Following the violence, Kennedy sent federal troops to defend Meredith and ensure that he enrolled successfully. However, once again the white protestors reacted violently and a riot broke out killing two people. Nonetheless, Meredith successfully enrolled. Although many white students shunned him, he graduated with a degree in Political Science in 1963.

Conclusion

The campaigns from 1955 to 1962 demonstrated the power of the civil rights movement. However, the Federal and state authorities remained reactive, responding to demands on a case-by-case basis without committing themselves to ending segregation once and for all.

Activity: Significance and success

1. Draw graph axes on a large piece of paper: label the *x*-axis 'date' and the *y*-axis 'significance'. Along the *x*-axis write the years from 1955–1962.
2. Write each protest in this chapter (including court cases) on a small card.
3. Place each card by the correct date on the *x*-axis.
4. Now reach a judgement about the significance of each of the protests. Consider: the extent to which they resulted in *de jure* and *de facto* change and their impact on the aims and methods of the civil rights movement. Move each small card up the *y*-axis to reflect your judgements. Do not fix the cards in place. Next to each card, write three bullet-points to explain your placement.
5. Now imagine that the *y*-axis is labelled 'Level of success'. Move your small cards accordingly. How is the arrangement different? Is the most significant protest always the most successful?

Chapter 7   Civil rights protests: the later southern campaigns, 1963–1965

Key questions
- How did the campaign methods used by the civil rights protestors develop in the period 1963–1965?
- What was achieved by the key protests of this period?
- Why were these protests significant?

How far would you go to win your freedom? Would you vote for change or start a court case? Would you organise a protest march or stop shopping in certain places? Would you break the law, go to court or risk imprisonment? Would you stand up against police with batons or water cannon? This chapter considers protestors who did all of these things in their fight for freedom.

Introduction

The civil rights campaigns from 1955 to 1962 targeted specific issues or specific localities. As the momentum grew, campaigners adopted a new slogan: 'Free by '63', indicating that the campaign was shifting to a national quest for freedom *now*.

The Birmingham Campaign (1963)

Why Birmingham?

Following the failure of the Albany Campaign (see Chapter 6, pages 39–40), Martin Luther King knew that he had to plan his next campaign carefully. In 1963, King focused his attention on Birmingham, Alabama, as the Freedom Rides had shown that the local Police Chief Eugene 'Bull' Connor would react violently to protest. As a result, widespread violence had broken out and the Federal Government had been forced to act. King hoped that a new campaign in Birmingham would provoke 'Bull' Connor and the ensuing violence would lead to the desegregation of the city.

King also targeted Birmingham because the city was one of the worst examples of segregation in the southern states. For example, Birmingham had no black police officers, bus drivers, fire-fighters or bank workers. Additionally, only 10 per cent of Birmingham's black population was registered to vote. Finally, the city authorities had banned the National Association for the Advancement of Colored People (NAACP), which showed how committed they were to maintaining segregation.

Goals for Birmingham

The campaign was organised by the Southern Christian Leadership Conference (SCLC). King set clear goals for the Birmingham Campaign

Take note

As you read through this chapter, add to the timeline you made for the last chapter. You may wish to record:
- the aims of the protests
- the methods used
- the civil rights groups involved
- the achievements of the protests.

Now use your notes to answer the following questions:
1. How far did the aims of the civil rights protestors change during this period?
2. How far did the methods of the civil rights protestors change during this period?

Try to make these notes follow on from those you made from the previous chapter. This will give you an annotated timeline of the period 1955–1965.

Source 7.1: Reverend Wyatt Tee Walker, one of the founders of the Southern Christian Leadership Conference (SCLC), describes his hopes for the Birmingham campaign.

My theory was that if we mounted a strong nonviolent movement, the opposition would surely do something to attract the media, and in turn induce national sympathy and attention to the everyday segregated circumstance of a person living in the Deep South.
Taken from: *Voices of Freedom* by Henry Hampton, Steve Fayer and Sarah Flynn (1990)

Source 7.2: An extract from King's *Letter from Birmingham Jail* criticising liberals who urged black people to show patience.

For years now I have heard the word 'Wait!' … This 'Wait' has almost always meant 'Never.' We must come to see, with one of our distinguished jurists, that 'justice too long delayed is justice denied'.

in order to avoid the apparent aimlessness of the Albany Campaign. The campaign focused on the desegregation of the city's major shopping areas, administrative buildings, schools and public parks, as well as demanding an end to racial discrimination in employment.

The progress of the Birmingham Campaign

Initially, 'Bull' Connor seemed to have changed his tactics. For example, he used legal methods, such as obtaining a court injunction against demonstrations in certain precincts, in order to weaken the protests. He also released high-profile campaigners such as jazz musician Al Hibbler in order to prevent negative media headlines. Nonetheless, King was arrested and jailed for taking part in an illegal march. While in prison he wrote his *Letter from Birmingham Jail* defending civil disobedience against those who said that black campaigners should work through the courts. King argued that he had the right to protest on the streets and break the law because a purely legal battle would never secure the rights of black people in America. King's letter, although written in April, was not published until June.

April, the first month of the campaign, was relatively calm. Consequently, in May the SCLC changed their tactics. James Bevel, a leading member of the SCLC, advocated recruiting students and young people to take part in the campaign. He argued that their imprisonment would not seriously affect the income of black families as they were not wage earners. Additionally, he believed that the Birmingham authorities would be embarrassed if their jails were full of young people. The subsequently recruited student marchers taunted the police, and as a result on 3 May, the police attacked demonstrators with high pressure fire hoses and arrested and imprisoned 1300 black children.

This caused a media frenzy. President John F. Kennedy said that he was 'sickened' by the images of police violence from Birmingham. Additionally, the Soviet media devoted one-fifth of their radio time to the protest. As far as the Soviet authorities were concerned the violence was clear evidence of American corruption and Soviet superiority. Kennedy was forced to act. He announced his support for a bill that would end segregation once and for all (see Chapter 9, page 53).

The significance of the Birmingham Campaign

'Bull' Connor's violent police tactics were the turning point in the campaign. Two days later, on 5 May, negotiations began between the SCLC and the city authorities. President Kennedy sent the assistant Attorney General to mediate. The negotiations led to the following reforms:

- Civil rights protestors were released from jail without charge.
- Large department stores were desegregated.
- Racial discrimination in employment was to be ended.

These were significant victories, but schools and most public places remained segregated. There was also much public opposition to desegregation in Birmingham. Four months after the end of the protest, members of the Ku Klux Klan bombed the **Sixteenth Street Baptist**

Church, killing four young girls and sparking demonstrations across Birmingham.

Nonetheless, the media coverage of the police violence had created greater sympathy for the civil rights movement among northern whites. More important still was President Kennedy's public commitment to support a Civil Rights Bill.

Criticisms of King

The Birmingham Campaign also resulted in criticisms of King and the SCLC. Some local black leaders felt that the SCLC had not worked with them and had ignored ongoing initiatives such as a boycott of segregated stores. Additionally, the SCLC was condemned for recruiting children and putting them in danger.

The March on Washington (1963)

In 1963 representatives from the SCLC, SNCC, CORE and the NAACP organised a march on Washington to commemorate the centenary of the Emancipation Proclamation (see Chapter 1, page 6). The march was designed to put pressure on the President and Congress to pass a Civil Rights Bill. King organised the march under the slogan 'For Jobs and Freedom'.

President Kennedy was unsure about the march. He feared that it would become violent and therefore jeopardise support for civil rights legislation. However, King assured Kennedy that the march would be peaceful. Notably, a significant minority of the marchers, approximately 20 per cent, were white. This show of unity indicated the level of popular support for civil rights legislation.

On 28 August, 250,000 people marched to the **Lincoln Memorial** to hear speeches from leading figures in the civil rights movement, along with those from religious and labour leaders. King spoke, delivering his famous 'I have a dream' speech.

The significance of the March on Washington

The March on Washington was significant in the following ways:
- It presented the civil rights movement as a united front, with common goals and methods.
- Despite Kennedy's fears, the march remained peaceful; this further increased white support for the civil rights movement.
- The nature and scale of the march attracted favourable media attention within the United States and abroad. A newspaper in Ghana reported that the march was among the 'greatest revolutions in the annals of human history'.
- The march solidified support for new civil rights legislation which would give the government the power to force southern states to desegregate.

Campaigning for voting rights

Following the successful passage of the 1964 Civil Rights Act (see Chapter 9, page 53), attention turned to voter registration and voting rights for black

Sixteenth Street Baptist Church

Birmingham's largest African-American church. The building was used as a headquarters for the civil rights movement during the Birmingham Campaign of 1963.

Lincoln Memorial

A building in Washington D.C. built to honour President Abraham Lincoln.

Source 7.3: Extract from Martin Luther King's 'I have a dream' speech, given at the Lincoln Memorial on 28 August 1963.

I have a dream that one day …. little black boys and black girls will be able to join hands with little white boys and white girls as sisters and brothers.

Glossary:

Voter registration campaign

Campaigns designed to increase the number of people registered to vote. People who are not registered to vote cannot vote.

Polling stations

A place where voters cast their votes.

people. The campaigns in Greenwood, Mississippi and Selma, Alabama, highlighted the need for further legislation to guarantee the voting rights of black people, leading to the Voting Rights Act of 1965.

Mississippi Freedom Summer (1964)

Activists from SNCC, CORE and the NAACP targeted Greenwood, Mississippi, for a **voter registration campaign**. Mississippi was targeted because it had the lowest black voter registration of any state. In 1962, only 6.2 per cent of adult black citizens were registered voters due to state laws that required potential voters to take literacy tests.

Approximately 800 volunteers from the North, many of whom were white, participated in the campaign. Activists attempted to increase voter registration by escorting black Americans to registration offices, sometimes with specially laid on bus services. Additionally, campaigners from SNCC and CORE established 30 'Freedom Schools' across Mississippi. These were designed to educate black citizens about civil rights issues and black history more generally, in order to encourage them to register to vote.

Student volunteers join together as they prepare for their involvement in the Mississippi Summer Project, 1964.

The local Ku Klux Klan and state police put up tremendous resistance to the voter registration campaign. For example, during the campaign, the homes of 30 black people and 37 black churches were firebombed. Additionally, there were 80 beatings, 35 shootings and over a thousand arrests. In June, Klansmen abducted and killed three civil rights workers – two white and one black. Civil rights volunteers were outraged. Notably, white juries in Mississippi refused to convict the men accused of this crime and it was not until 2005, 41 years later, that the men were found guilty.

During the Freedom Summer campaign, approximately 17,000 black people tried to register to vote in Mississippi. However, police intimidation, Klan violence and the unwillingness of local authorities to co-operate with black citizens meant that only 1600 succeeded in registering.

Black people were also turned away from **polling stations** during the Democratic Primary for the Presidential election of 1964. As a result, activists set up the Mississippi Freedom Democratic Party (MFDP), which held its own Primary. This resulted in two Primary elections: the **'lily-white'** Democratic Party primary and the Mississippi Freedom Democratic Party primary. Both of these primaries elected delegates to the forthcoming Democratic Party Congress, which would nominate the Presidential candidate for the 1964 Presidential election.

President Johnson proposed a compromise: the 'lily-white' delegates would be the official delegates, but the MFDP delegates would be honoured guests who could attend the conference but have no voting rights. The

MFDP delegates rejected the compromise. Led by **Fannie Lou Hamer**, the Freedom Democrats arrived at the Congress in Atlanta demanding to be accepted as Mississippi's official delegates.

The controversy over the Mississippi Freedom Summer and the MFDP was significant because it signalled a breakdown in the relationship between civil rights campaigners and President Johnson. Additionally, many civil rights activists saw this as proof that the American political system was fundamentally racist and that it was therefore necessary to use more militant methods and to stop compromising with white politicians.

Selma Campaign (1965)

The Selma Campaign, like the Mississippi Freedom Summer, was part of an ongoing campaign to register black people to vote. The SCLC focused on Selma, Alabama, because only 1 per cent of black adults were registered to vote. Additionally, King believed that the local Sheriff Jim Clark was likely to respond to a civil rights campaign with violence.

SCLC and SNCC activists held a series of demonstrations to raise publicity for the campaign. The local police responded violently; in one case, police used electric cattle prods against protestors. The police were also responsible for the murder of Jimmie Lee Jackson, a 26-year-old black man who had been protecting his mother and grandmother from a brutal police beating.

The climax of the Selma Campaign was a 50-mile march from Selma to Montgomery. Montgomery was chosen as the destination for the march in order to mark the tenth anniversary of the Montgomery Bus Boycott.

The first attempt to stage the march ended just outside Selma when the police, armed with bullwhips and tear gas, forced the marchers to turn back at the Edmund Pettus Bridge. The second attempt two days later, on 9 March, was also unsuccessful. Under pressure from President Johnson, King took the decision to turn back again at the Edmund Pettus Bridge. Finally, on 21 March, 8000 people began a five-day march from Selma to Montgomery. By the time they arrived in Montgomery, four days later, their numbers had increased to 25,000, indicating the extent of support for the voting rights campaign.

The significance of the campaigns for voting rights

The voting campaigns of the mid-1960s were significant in the following ways:

- They highlighted the problems faced by black people in asserting their right to vote and therefore led to the Voting Rights Act of 1965.
- Once again media images of opposition to civil rights increased support for the movement.

> ### Glossary:
> ### 'Lily-white'
> An informal term used to describe a group or process that excludes black people.

> ### Fannie Lou Hamer
> ### (1917–1977)
> Civil rights campaigner and member of SNCC. She was a committed Christian who believed she had a religious duty to stand up for justice. She was well known for speaking her mind frankly. She took part in the Mississippi Freedom Summer, and later, Martin Luther King's Poor People's Campaign.

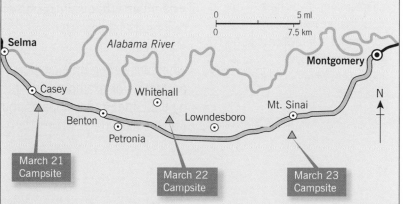

Route of the Selma to Montgomery march, 1965.

- They initially showed a high degree of co-operation between CORE, SNCC and the SCLC.
- They led to criticism of King for co-operating with President Johnson and ending the second march to Montgomery.
- They revealed growing tensions within the civil rights movement over the extent to which black campaigners could trust and work with the Federal Government.

Conclusion

More than a century after the Emancipation Proclamation which announced the freedom of slaves, American politicians finally enacted laws that would lead to the end of formal racial inequality. This was a massive *de jure* victory for the civil rights campaign. Nonetheless, the Civil Rights Act (see Chapter 9, page 53) did not mark an end to the struggle and campaigners now focused their attention to bringing about *de facto* change.

Activity: Changing methods

Taking it further

The years covered in this chapter are often viewed as the high point of the civil rights movement. In particular, the March on Washington in 1963 is seen as an example that the movement was united, powerful and effective in generating change. However, this was also the period in which tensions between the civil rights groups increased. What evidence can you find in this chapter (and, if you have time, the previous chapter) to indicate that relationships within the civil rights movement were becoming strained?

1. Throughout the period 1955–1968, civil rights protestors changed and developed their methods in response to the successes and failures of their campaigns. The Birmingham Campaign is especially notable for the way in which the protestors drew on the experiences of previous campaigns.

   In the centre of a large piece of paper, write 'The Birmingham Campaign'. Around the edge of the piece of paper, write the names of all previous nonviolent protests:

   the Montgomery Bus Boycott, Little Rock, the Sit-ins, the Freedom Rides and Albany.

   Draw links from these campaigns to the Birmingham Campaign to show how Birmingham was influenced by previous campaigns. For example, the first link you draw could show that the technique of nonviolent direct action used in Montgomery was also used in Birmingham. Make sure that you annotate your diagram to explain your links.

2. The American historian S. Jonathan Bass has stated 'the Birmingham movement was a culmination of all King's ideas, theology, experiences and civil rights tactics'. Use your diagram to explain how far you agree with this statement.

   When answering the question, remember that King was not involved in all of the protests. For example, it is fine to draw the conclusion that King was influenced by the Little Rock campaign, but remember that he was not involved in its organisation.

Chapter 8   Martin Luther King's last campaigns

Key questions

- Why did Martin Luther King begin to campaign in the North?
- What were the aims and methods of his northern campaigns?
- How successful were his northern campaigns?

By 1965, many white Americans felt that the civil rights movement had become obsolete. Segregation had been outlawed and voting rights had been guaranteed. Indeed, when Martin Luther King was awarded the Nobel Peace Prize in 1964, he stated that as a result of his campaigns 'an **obdurate**, centuries-old, and traditional conflict is now nearing its solution'.

However, King knew that racial equality required more than just legal change. He therefore turned his attention to the social and economic problems of the northern states. His campaigns in the North were to prove the most difficult of his career.

Timeline

1965	Moynihan Report published
1966	Chicago Freedom Movement
1968	Memphis Workers' Strike
	4 April: Martin Luther King assassinated

Glossary:

Obdurate

Stubborn; obstinate; unmoving.

Why did King's focus move to the northern states?

The 1964 Civil Rights Act (see Chapter 9, page 53) outlawed segregation in the southern states of America. However, it did little to address the problems faced by black Americans in the northern states. These states had not imposed legal segregation, but racial discrimination in social and economic forms still existed. In 1965, the Moynihan Report was published investigating the extent of social and economic discrimination against black Americans. This influential report inspired Martin Luther King to make this form of discrimination the focus of his next campaign.

Daniel Patrick Moynihan

(1927–2003)

Socialist and Democratic Senator for New York and US Ambassador to the United Nations.

The Moynihan Report (1965)

The Negro Family: The Case for National Action, also known as the Moynihan Report, was a study of the economic position of black Americans by **Daniel Patrick Moynihan**. The report drew attention to the high levels of crime within the black community and the poor living conditions of many black families. It also noted that ghettoisation in the North was leading to *de facto* segregation of education and housing.

Take note

As you read this section make brief notes on:
- the contents of the Moynihan Report
- the significance of the Moynihan Report.

Take note

As you read through this section, answer the following questions:

1. What were King's aims for the Chicago protest?
2. How did he plan to protest in Chicago?
3. In what ways could the Chicago campaign be viewed as a success?
4. In what ways could the Chicago campaign be viewed as a failure?
5. How did the Chicago campaign change King's attitude to protest in the North?

President Johnson, who had commissioned the report, hoped to use it to promote economic equality. However, this idea backfired. Black leaders were horrified because the report blamed black people for their economic problems and suggested that they were incapable of helping themselves. The report was significant for two reasons:

- It created further tension between well-meaning liberal politicians such as President Johnson and black radicals.
- It was used by some whites to argue against government help for black people.

The Chicago Freedom Movement (1966)

The Chicago Freedom Movement represented the alliance of the Southern Christian Leadership Conference (SCLC) and the Coordinating Council of Community Organizations (CCCO). The Chicago campaign was King's first initiative in the North. He aimed to use the techniques of nonviolent direct action that had been so successfully employed in the South to challenge the *de facto* segregation of Chicago's education, housing and employment.

The first rally, on 10 June 1966, was disappointing as only 30,000 people attended rather than the 100,000 King had expected. Even so, events soon escalated. A heatwave led people in black neighbourhoods to use fire hydrants to cool themselves. The authorities demanded that the fire hydrants should be shut off to preserve water in case of a fire, and when police arrived to enforce this a riot erupted. Chicago Mayor, Richard Daley, made matters worse by cutting off water to the fire hydrants in the west side ghetto. King organised a meeting to appeal for calm, but the violence intensified.

Following the riots, King tried to engage Chicago's black community in peaceful protest. He targeted segregated housing, organising marches through all-white areas. Chicago's whites fought back. At the Gage Park March, King was bombarded with rocks and over 1000 police officers were unable to subdue the violent white crowds. King told the press 'I have never seen – even in Mississippi and Alabama – mobs as hostile and hate-filled as I've seen in Chicago'. However, worse violence looked likely. **Jesse Jackson**, one of the leaders of the SCLC, planned more marches through white areas known for their racism. Chicago Police Chief Richard B. Ogilvie warned that they would 'make Gage Park look like a tea party'.

The threat of increased violence forced Mayor Daley to negotiate. However, he also obtained a court injunction severely restricting future marches. The court order changed the balance of power at the negotiations and King was forced to compromise. The Chicago Real Estate Board, which was responsible for overseeing Chicago's housing, promised to respect the city's fair housing laws. King presented the compromise as a victory, but local black leaders were less optimistic. Indeed, following Daley's re-election as Mayor in 1967, promises of fair housing were ignored.

The significance of Chicago

King's apparent failure in Chicago was significant because it led to further criticism of his leadership and tactics:

- Local CORE activists claimed that King had made tactical mistakes in the campaign, such as his decision not to break the court injunction restricting further marches.
- Many of Chicago's black citizens lost faith in the SCLC and turned to more radical black leadership.

The campaign also highlighted the extent to which King had misjudged the situation in the North:

- The campaign had revealed a 'white backlash' against greater racial equality.
- White labour unions failed to support the campaign.
- The campaign failed to win the support of the churches.
- Black church leaders in the North had relatively small congregations and did not command the respect of the Chicago black community. Consequently, King's Christian philosophy and commitment to nonviolent protest had far fewer supporters.
- President Johnson refused to involve the Federal Government in the campaign because he was no longer willing to work with King following his attack on the Vietnam War (see Chapter 17, page 102).

Finally, the campaign revealed the scale of the problems faced by black people in the North:

- Chicago was ten times bigger than Birmingham and one hundred times bigger than Selma. Some of the black ghettos themselves were bigger than entire southern towns.
- Segregation had been ended in the South by changing the law. In contrast, social and economic change required high levels of financial investment; authorities were reluctant to commit money to addressing these problems.
- King admitted that urban regeneration could not be solved quickly and might take at least ten years.

The problems of Chicago were common to many of the northern cities, and forced King to rethink his strategy.

The Poor People's Campaign (1968)

In response to Chicago, King planned the Poor People's Campaign (PPC). This marked a radicalisation of his approach. King aimed to create a coalition big enough to tackle the social and economic problems identified during the Chicago campaign. This coalition would include black people, Puerto Ricans, Mexicans, American Indians and poor white people. Together, they would campaign for a better standard of living for the poor and an end to the ghettos. The campaign's strategy would be nationwide civil disobedience, occupying government buildings, boycotting businesses and, finally, a march on Washington. The campaigners would demand:

- a federal budget of $30 billion a year to combat poverty
- a government commitment to full employment
- government initiatives to build half a million new houses a year.

The campaign reflected the fact that King had changed his mind about American politics. In his early campaigns he had believed that he could work

Take note

As you read through this section make notes on the following spider diagram:

49

James Earl Ray

(1928–1998)

Prior to the assassination of King, Ray was a petty criminal. He was convicted because his fingerprints were found on a gun discovered near to the scene of the murder. Ray initially confessed to the crime, but retracted his confession soon after. He maintained his innocence for the rest of his life but most historians believe he was guilty.

Take note

As you read through this section make bullet-pointed notes on:
1. King's reasons for supporting the strike
2. the events of the strike
3. the strike's impact on King
4. the significance of King's assassination.

Moses

The leader of the Jewish nation who led the Jewish people out of slavery in Egypt to the Promised Land. Moses never entered the Promised Land but he was able to see it from the top of a mountain before he died.

within the system. The Chicago campaign had taught him that more radical demands, coupled with more radical methods, were needed to ensure real change.

However, King's new plans faced enormous problems. President Johnson made it clear that he did not support the plan. The Vietnam War had created a split between civil rights radicals and liberal politicians, including President Johnson. Additionally it had diverted resources from social projects designed to promote social justice. Nonetheless, by March 1968 SCLC's organisers had won the support of many Labour Unions and religious groups and had begun to raise the money necessary to run the campaign.

The Memphis Sanitation Workers' Strike (1968)

King's attention was diverted away from plans for the PPC by the Memphis Sanitation Workers' Strike. The Memphis city authorities refused to recognise the workers' union and used tear gas to break up their marches. To some extent the protest was an example of the kind of campaign King wanted to organise. The Sanitation Workers' Union was largely black but also included some poor whites. Moreover, their goals were economic: they aimed to increase their income. Finally, their protests were nonviolent. As a result, when King was asked to lend his support he agreed.

The Memphis campaign was not a success. The peaceful march, which King helped to lead, lasted less than an hour. Marchers themselves began attacking shops and looting, and the police responded with tear gas. Some papers reported that King had led a violent march, while others branded him a chicken for fleeing as soon as the march turned violent. King knew that these headlines jeopardised the PPC because his reputation was crucial to winning support for the campaign.

King, Jackson and other leading members of the SCLC tried to turn defeat into victory by staging another march. However, before this was possible King was assassinated. He was shot on 4 April by **James Earl Ray** while standing on the balcony of his Memphis hotel room. He died at the age of 39.

> **Source 8.2: Martin Luther King's final speech, given the day before he died. His words, a reference to the Biblical figure Moses, seem to anticipate his fate.**
>
> I've seen the Promised Land. I may not get there with you. But … we, as a people, will get to the Promised Land.

The significance of King's assassination

King's death became a symbol of the end of the civil rights movement, at least as it had been known in the 1950s and 1960s. President Johnson called for a national day of mourning and the authorities in Memphis gave in to the demands of the Memphis Sanitation Workers. More than 50,000 mourners joined King's funeral procession. Black Americans reacted violently. Racial

Destruction caused by Chicago riots following Martin Luther King's assassination in 1968 – this is all that remained of the west side business district.

violence broke out in 130 cities across 29 states. SNCC leader Stokely Carmichael summed up the feeling behind the violence in the following words: 'When white America killed Dr King, she declared war on us... Black people have to survive, and the only way they will survive is by getting a gun.'

Activity: North v. South

Martin Luther King's campaigns in the North were undoubtedly less successful than his campaigns in the South. In order to assess the reasons for this, carry out the following tasks:

1. Take a large sheet of paper. On the left-hand side of the sheet, list the reasons why King's campaigns in the South were so successful.

2. On the right-hand side of the sheet, list the reasons why King's campaigns in the North were less successful.

3. Now draw lines between your two lists, showing how the circumstances of the campaigns changed when King moved his focus to the North. Next to each line write a brief comment to explain why this change made the campaigns less successful. Your notes from these first three steps may look something like this:

Reasons for success in the South
Widespread support from
black people
Lots of media attention

Reasons for failure in the North
Increased violence
Lack of support from
black people

Black people in the North were less supportive of King's nonviolent tactics.

4. Use your completed diagram to plan an answer to the question 'Why were Martin Luther King's campaigns in the North less successful than those in the South?'

Taking it further

It is easy to find fault with Martin Luther King's northern campaigns: public support was low; peaceful protest turned to violence; aims were not met; the Federal Government was uncooperative. However, it is unfair to view these campaigns as an unmitigated disaster. Use the information in this chapter to list three ways in which the northern campaigns could be viewed as a success. For each, make a general point and then support this point with specific examples. Finish each paragraph by explaining how your point suggests the campaigns were successful.

Chapter 9 The role of the federal government

Key questions

- How far did the Presidents of this period promote civil rights?
- What were the key features of the civil rights acts passed during this period?
- What role was played by Congress and the Supreme Court in promoting civil rights?

Prior to 1963 successive American Presidents seemed reluctant to use their power to deliver civil rights. The turning point was 1963, the year in which every surviving President publicly backed the bill that became the 1964 Civil Rights Act.

Timeline

President:	Major civil rights legislation:	Date:
President Dwight D. Eisenhower (1953–1961)	Civil Rights Act passed	1957
	Civil Rights Act passed	1960
President John F. Kennedy (1961–1963)	Civil Rights Act initiated	
President Lyndon B. Johnson (1963–1969)	Civil Rights Act passed	1964
	Voting Rights Act passed	1965
	Civil Rights Act (Fair Housing Act) passed	1968

Take note

Make a copy of the timeline above. As you read through the following sections, add information to the timeline to show:
a) whether each President was a Republican or a Democrat
b) the attitude of each President towards civil rights (summarise this information in no more than 3 bullet points)
c) the key features of each of the Civil Rights Acts passed during this period.

Introduction

The federal government is headed by the President, but it also comprises Congress and the Supreme Court, each of which had a role to play in dismantling segregation.

The Presidents

Eisenhower, Kennedy and Johnson all initiated or passed Civil Rights Acts. In addition to the acts shown on the timeline, President Johnson also passed two acts that improved access to education for black students. Notably, civil rights was not the only issue on their agenda and therefore it did not receive their full attention.

Dwight D. Eisenhower (1953–1961), Republican

Eisenhower believed that the position of black people would improve of its own accord over time. In this sense he did not think that it was the government's job to improve conditions for black people. This general approach is evident in his reluctance to become involved in Little Rock in 1957 (see Chapter 6, page 37). Nonetheless, towards the end of his presidency, Eisenhower proposed two Civil Rights Acts. Notably, both Acts faced considerable opposition in Congress and the terms of the Acts were weakened as a result (see Chapter 10).

Civil Rights Act of 1957

This Act focused on the voting rights of African Americans. The Act proposed the establishment of a Commission on Civil Rights – a **bi-partisan** committee designed to monitor the voting rights of America's black citizens. However, individuals found guilty of preventing black Americans from registering as voters would face a fine of only $1000 or a maximum sentence of six months in jail. These penalties were relatively small and did not act as a deterrent.

Civil Rights Act of 1960

This Act narrowly extended the powers of the Commission on Civil Rights by requiring local authorities to keep records of voter registration. This allowed the Commission to monitor black voter registration more accurately. By 1960, Eisenhower's two Acts had only increased the proportion of black voters by 3 per cent.

John F. Kennedy (1961–1963), Democrat

During his election campaign, Kennedy claimed that he was sympathetic to the plight of black Americans. For example, he made a highly publicised telephone call to **Coretta King** while her husband was in prison during the sit-in protests of 1960. He also promised a civil rights act to end segregation.

Despite his promises, Kennedy was slow to use his power to help black people. Initially, Kennedy did little to advance racial equality because he needed the support of southern white politicians in Congress. His early moves were largely symbolic. For example, he appointed five black judges to the federal courts, including the NAACP's chief counsel Thurgood Marshall. In addition, he created the Committee on Equal Employment Opportunity (CEEO), which was designed to ensure equal employment opportunities for everyone who worked for the federal government. However, very few black people were employed by the federal government and therefore the measure had little impact.

The Birmingham Campaign of March 1963 (see Chapter 7, pages 41–43) forced Kennedy to show decisive leadership and fulfil his promise of a civil rights act. But it was not until the March on Washington in August 1963 that he threw his weight behind the Civil Rights Bill.

Lyndon B. Johnson (1963–1969), Democrat

Following Kennedy's assassination in November 1963, his Vice-President Lyndon B. Johnson became America's new President. Johnson saw the Civil Rights Act as part of a range of measures collectively known as the 'Great Society', which were designed to make America a fairer place. Prior to becoming President, Johnson had had a mixed record on civil rights. For example, although he had used his position as an American senator to support both of Eisenhower's Civil Rights Acts, he also played a key role in watering them down.

Civil Rights Act of 1964

The Act explicitly outlawed the segregation of any facility or public place. It gave the Commission on Civil Rights the power to enforce desegregation and it made the Fair Employment Practices Commission (see Chapter 11, page 62), permanent. In general terms, the Act spelled the end of legal segregation across the South (see Chapter 11).

Voting Rights Act of 1965

The Act explicitly outlawed all 'tests' that prevented any American citizen

Glossary:
Bi-partisan
Representing both of the main political parties.

Coretta King
(1927–2006)
The wife of Martin Luther King. Coretta King was born in Alabama and attended segregated schools. She met Martin Luther King while studying in Boston and they married in 1953. She took part in the Montgomery Bus Boycott and supported her husband in all subsequent protests. Following Martin Luther King's death, she continued to campaign for civil rights, broadening her focus to include the rights of women, homosexuals and the poor. She also travelled to South Africa to campaign against apartheid. When she died in 2006, 14,000 people attended her funeral.

from voting. Additionally, the Act gave the federal government the power to oversee voting registration across America. Consequently, it ended the ability of local governments to deny black citizens their right to vote. Again, this was far more effective than previous legislation (see Chapter 11).

Elementary and Secondary Education Act (1965) and Higher Education Act (1965)

These Acts increased the funding given to education. Money was targeted to help the poorest states, the poorest schools and the poorest students. Consequently, the Acts helped southern states, schools with a high proportion of black students and individual black students at college or university.

Civil Rights Act of 1968 (Fair Housing Act)

This Act outlawed discrimination of any form in the sale or rental of housing. In this sense, it attempted to address the issue of ghettoisation. However, the Act gave the government no new powers to enforce the law and consequently the Act's impact was limited.

Johnson's early measures on civil rights were highly effective. However, the Vietnam War dominated Johnson's attention (see Chapter 18, pages 101–104) and claimed a growing proportion of government resources. Additionally, King's public criticisms of the war drove a wedge between the SCLC and the Johnson government. As a result, civil rights were less of a priority in the second half of Johnson's period in office.

The role of Congress and the Supreme Court

Congress

Congress is the body empowered by the American Constitution to create nationwide laws. Consequently, Congress's support was essential for progress in terms of civil rights legislation. However, the southern states had a significant voice in Congress and as a result southern senators and congressmen obstructed civil rights legislation from 1945 to 1960. However, in 1964, 73 out of America's 100 senators and 289 of the 435 members of the House of Representatives voted in favour of the Civil Rights Act.

Congress's attitude to civil rights legislation changed for five reasons:
- Grass-roots campaigns, such as the Birmingham Campaign of 1963, exposed the horrors of segregation and racial violence.
- The civil rights campaigns had won over public support to such an extent that Congress could no longer oppose the Civil Rights Bill.
- Johnson was an experienced politician and knew how to exploit Congress to ensure that the Bill passed. For example, he persuaded important members of Congress, such as the Republican Leader in the Senate, Everett Dirksen, to support the Bill.
- Following the 1964 Congressional elections, some conservative southern Democrats were replaced by more liberal Democrats who were sympathetic to civil rights.
- Johnson persuaded Congress that the Act would be a fitting legacy for Kennedy.

The Supreme Court

During the 1950s, the Supreme Court showed considerable leadership on

---

Take note

This section considers the role of Congress and the Supreme Court in the struggle for civil rights. Copy the following table and use the information in this section to complete it. Add specific examples and dates where possible.

	Congress	The Supreme Court
What is the role of this body? (See Chapter 1)		
How did this body help or hinder the campaign for civil rights?		
Why did it act in this way?		

civil rights issues. Eisenhower's 1953 decision to appoint Earl Warren as Chief Justice of the Supreme Court was extremely important (see Chapter 5, page 29). Supreme Court decisions in cases such as *Brown v. Board of Education of Topeka* (1954), *Brown II* (1955) and *Browder v. Gayle* (1956) picked apart the legal basis of segregation (see Chapters 5 and 6). Civil rights activists were then able to use these rulings to force change in campaigns such as the sit-ins across the southern states of America.

Conclusion

During the 1950s the Supreme Court used its power to support desegregation. Nonetheless, without the support of the President or Congress it could not guarantee that *de jure* change resulted in *de facto* change. The support of Congress and the President in the mid-1960s was necessary to ensure the final destruction of segregation.

Activity: Compelled to act?

In this chapter you have studied the actions of the Presidents in the period 1953–1968. In Chapters 6, 7 and 8 you studied the actions of the civil rights movement during this period. In order to understand better the links between these two strands, complete the following activity.

1. Copy the following timeline (your timeline should be at least A3 size):

	1953	1954	1955	1956	1957	1958	1959	1960	1961	1962	1963	1964	1965	1966	1967	1968
Federal government action																
Civil rights movement protests																

2. Using your notes from this chapter and Chapters 6, 7 and 8, add key events to your timeline. For example, on the top row mark down the changes of President and the civil rights acts. On the bottom row note down the key protests.

3. Add detail to your timelines. For example, explain what the civil rights protests achieved.

4. Using a different coloured pen, draw lines to show links between the events on the timeline. For example, President Eisenhower was forced to intervene in the Little Rock protest.

5. Ensure that as well as marking each link on the timeline, you also write a brief explanation of the nature of the link.

6. Discuss: How far were the actions of the federal government a result of the actions of the civil rights protestors? How far were the actions of the civil rights protestors a result of the actions (or inaction) or the federal government?

Taking it further

In his book *Harry Truman and Civil Rights: Moral Courage and Political Risks* (2003), the lawyer and historian Michael R. Gardner argues that President Truman – more than Presidents Eisenhower, Kennedy and Johnson – should be congratulated for his record on civil rights. He claims that while Presidents Eisenhower, Kennedy and Johnson were forced to take action to protect their political careers, Truman was under no such pressure and acted only because he 'felt [it] was morally right'.

Look back at your work on President Truman in Chapter 3. How far do you agree with Gardner's conclusion? In reaching a judgement, remember to assess not only Truman's motivation but also that of Eisenhower, Kennedy and Johnson.

Chapter 10 **Opposition to change, 1955–1968**

Key questions

- Which groups and individuals opposed the civil rights movement?
- What methods did they use to oppose the movement?
- How effective was their opposition?

Senator Robert Byrd of West Virginia is currently the longest-serving member of the American Senate. He was elected in 1959 and has been re-elected at every election ever since. His political career, however, started in 1942 when he joined the Ku Klux Klan. Byrd used his political position in the Senate to oppose civil rights, working tirelessly to try to defeat the 1964 Civil Rights Act. Byrd has since apologised for his racism. Nonetheless, he was not alone in his opposition to the Civil Rights Act. Indeed, throughout this period, many groups and individuals sought to disrupt the progress of the civil rights movement.

Take note

1. As you read through this chapter, make notes on the form and effectiveness of opposition to the civil rights movement between 1955 and 1968. The notes can be in any form you wish, but remember that the purpose of note-taking is to capture important information in a clear and organised way.
2. Swap notes with a partner. Assess your partner's notes in terms of:
   a) organisation
   b) clarity
   c) choice of material.
3. List three good points about your partner's note-taking skills.
4. List two ways in which your partner could improve his or her note-taking skills.

Introduction

Opposition to racial justice came from a variety of different individuals, groups and institutions. At a federal level this included the President, Congress, the Supreme Court and the FBI, while at a local and state level, state governors, city mayors and local police were often violently opposed to civil rights campaigns. Outside the realm of political institutions and public officials, white racists organised themselves in a variety of ways.

Federal opposition to civil rights

Presidential opposition

None of the Presidents in the period 1955–1968 was opposed to the objectives of the civil rights campaigns. Nonetheless, all of the Presidents opposed their methods.

President Eisenhower (1953–1961) rarely took the initiative on civil rights issues. His general view was that black campaigns would do more harm than good because they would cause resentment among America's white population. He believed that black people needed to be patient and in time change would come. This point of view, however, ignored the daily injustice of racism in America.

President John F. Kennedy (1961–1963) was more proactive than Eisenhower. Nonetheless, he too disagreed with the methods of the campaigners.

- Kennedy was horrified by the violence caused by the Freedom Rides of 1961 and called for the campaign to stop (see Chapter 6, page 39). Following the Freedom Rides he encouraged civil rights campaigners to abandon protests and to put their efforts into voter registration.

- Kennedy set up the Voter Education Project (VEP) in 1962. VEP offered grants to groups of activists who would abandon direct action to focus on voter registration.
- Prior to 1963 Kennedy tried to keep the federal government out of the struggle. For example, he resisted calls to send federal troops to protect protestors during the Freedom Rides. It was only after the Birmingham Campaign of 1963 that Kennedy was prepared to support a civil rights bill.

President Lyndon B. Johnson (1963–1969) was the most radical of the Presidents during this period. Between 1963 and 1965 he worked with civil rights campaigners to bring about change. However, once civil rights leaders criticised his policies in Vietnam he distanced himself from the campaign. He was critical of Martin Luther King's Chicago campaign of 1966 and did not support the proposed Poor People's Campaign of 1968. By the end of the 1960s, Johnson, like Kennedy before him, took the view that King's campaigns were too provocative and that further voter registration, rather than direct action, was the key to better conditions for black Americans.

Opposition from Congress

An alliance of southern Democrats and many Republicans did much to weaken the Civil Rights Acts of 1957, 1960 and 1968. For example, Democratic Senator James Strom Thurmond staged the longest one-person **filibuster** in American history to try and kill the 1957 bill – he spoke continually for 24 hours and 18 minutes. Similarly, a group of 18 southern Democrats working in teams kept a filibuster going for over 125 hours to block Eisenhower's 1960 Civil Rights Bill. Finally, Congress weakened the 1968 Civil Rights Act in such a way that the new rights it promised could not be enforced by the federal government. Nonetheless, Congress did back the Civil Rights Act of 1964 and the Voting Rights Act of 1965 which gave the government significant power to force desegregation and support voter registration.

The FBI

The **FBI** used its power to undermine the civil rights movement on many occasions in the 1950s and 1960s. J. Edgar Hoover, the head of the FBI from 1924 to 1972, was a dedicated anti-Communist. Hoover suspected civil rights organisations, such as the NAACP, the SCLC, the SNCC and CORE, had links to the Communist Party and therefore posed a threat to American democracy. Consequently, he set up COINTELPRO – the Counter Intelligence Program – to investigate radical groups. COINTELPRO's tactics included spying on civil rights groups, breaking into their offices and harassing civil rights activists. However, its main tactic was infiltration, a process whereby COINTELPRO agents would join groups such as the SNCC posing as civil rights activists and encourage disagreement and rivalry in order to weaken the groups from within.

State and local government

Local politicians

Local politicians were generally more strongly opposed to racial justice than national politicians. State Governors often did everything within their power

Glossary:
Filibuster

A technique used by members of Congress to obstruct the passage of legislation. A member of Congress or a team working together will make speeches continuously, using up all the time allocated to the bill. As a result, Congress cannot vote on the bill and it cannot be passed into law.

Glossary:
FBI

The Federal Bureau of Investigation is a police agency that investigates crimes that cross state boundaries. In this sense it is America's national police force.

to resist change. Governor Orval Faubus, for example, used a combination of violence, propaganda and legal measures to stop the integration of Little Rock Central High School in 1957 (see Chapter 6, page 37). He was aided by local state law makers who passed new laws allowing him to close schools rather than desegregate them. He also used state funds to pay for lawyers to fight against desegregation.

Local politicians in the North were also opposed to civil rights campaigns. Indeed, Mayor Richard J. Daley proved to be particularly effective at preventing progress in the Chicago campaign of 1966 (see Chapter 8, page 48). Daley's tactics were more sophisticated than those of Faubus. Daley publically agreed to negotiate with King. However, behind the scenes his lawyers managed to legally prohibit further large-scale protests. Daley also made a series of impressive promises. However, once the campaign was over and his position was secure, he did little to implement them.

Local police

Police forces in the southern states were some of the main obstacles to racial equality in the 1950s and 1960s. They adopted a variety of tactics to oppose the civil rights campaign. For example, in Birmingham in 1963, Eugene 'Bull' Connor authorised the use of water cannon as a weapon against the protests (see Chapter 7, page 42). Connor's tactics were counterproductive and led to significant civil rights victories because the violence attracted media attention which in turn forced the federal government to support the protests. However, police violence did not always aid the protestors. Indeed, police use of tear gas and batons in Memphis in 1968 (see Chapter 8, page 50) did not provoke government action. Albany Police Chief Laurie Pritchett used more sophisticated methods during the Albany campaign of 1961–1962 (see Chapter 6, page 39). By ensuring that the police behaved in a respectful manner, Pritchett denied protestors the media attention they needed to force the federal government to take action. Northern police were also an obstacle to the civil rights campaign. In Chicago in 1966, for example, the police's attempts to enforce the closure of fire hydrants led to a riot (see Chapter 8, page 48).

Public opinion

Public opinion was a significant barrier to racial equality in the late 1960s. In general terms the majority of Americans supported an end to legal segregation. However, the majority of whites did not want to live in integrated neighbourhoods. This is obvious from the phenomenon of '**white flight**': the white population of America's major cities declined by 9.6 per cent between 1960 and 1970. Indeed, in 1968 alone, 16.8 per cent of the white population left America's biggest northeastern cities for the suburbs. Moreover, those leaving were overwhelmingly the well-off high status professionals. As a result, the tax revenues of America's cities declined and therefore the provision of public services suffered, further disadvantaging urban black communities. Opposition to economic equality and fair housing was also obvious in the violent reaction of many of Chicago's whites to King's Chicago campaign of 1966 (see Chapter 8, page 48).

Glossary:

White flight

The movement of white people from racially desegregated residential areas to those populated exclusively by white people.

Conclusion

There were many obstacles to racial justice in the 1950s and 1960s. Indeed, the civil rights movement faced opposition as it tried to change laws, ensure these laws were enforced and address issues of social and economic equality. The fact that the civil rights movement continued to campaign for change, even in the face of such opposition, is testament to the courage, strength and commitment of its members.

Activity: Helping or hindering?

It is beyond doubt that those who opposed the civil rights movement were trying to hinder progress towards equal rights in America. However, it is possible to argue that many, inadvertently, aided the movement. Indeed, following the Birmingham Campaign, President Kennedy famously declared that 'The civil rights movement should thank God for Bull Connor. He's helped it as much as Abraham Lincoln'.

1. In order to assess the extent to which opposition to civil rights actually aided the civil rights campaign, use the information in this chapter to complete the following table. (Note: there may not be evidence to complete every box – just add evidence where possible.)

   Remember to add specific examples wherever possible.

Source of opposition	Ways in which this type of opposition hindered the civil rights campaigns	Ways in which this type of opposition helped the civil rights campaigns
Federal opposition		
Local government		
Public opinion		

2. Having completed the table, use the information to write an answer to the following question: 'How far do you agree that opposition to the civil rights movement did more to help the movement than to hinder it?'

   Your answer must be carefully structured and must provide evidence to support your points. Although it is important that you present a balanced argument, remember to reach a judgement in your introduction and to stick to it throughout the essay.

3. In order to check that you have maintained your argument throughout your answer, allow a partner to read your introduction and your conclusion and check that you have reached the same judgement in both parts of the essay.

Taking it further

In previous chapters you have studied how the methods used by civil rights protestors changed and developed in the period 1955–1968. In many ways, these changes were caused by opposition to the movement.

1. Make a simple flowchart showing how the methods used by the civil rights campaigners changed in this period. For example, your diagram could begin by showing the transition from court cases, such as *Brown v. Board of Education*, to nonviolent protest such as the Montgomery Bus Boycott.

2. Where possible, explain how this change in methods was a response to different levels and forms of opposition.

Chapter 11 The achievements of peaceful protest

Key questions
- How far had racial equality been achieved by 1968?
- How had public opinion towards civil rights changed by 1968?

Michelle Obama was two years old when Martin Luther King began his campaign in Chicago. She lived with her family in Chicago's South Side, a working-class black neighbourhood. She attended high school then Princeton University before becoming a lawyer and then, in 2009, America's First Lady. Her story has been described as a modern version of the American dream. Michelle Obama herself notes that her 'piece of the American Dream is a blessing hard won by those who came before me'. By this she means that her story was only possible thanks to the achievements of campaigners who fought for racial justice in the generations since her family was first brought to America as slaves.

Take note

Use this table to summarise the information in this chapter. Remember to include specific information where possible (examiners love statistics!).

	What had been achieved?	Limitations of change
Education		
Transport		
Public places		
Voting rights		
Employment and income		
Housing		
Public support for civil rights		

The achievements of the civil rights movement

By 1968, full racial equality had not been achieved. Nonetheless, significant progress had been made in terms of education, transport, desegregation of public places, voting rights, employment and public opinion. Housing, however, remained a significant problem which successive government initiatives had failed to solve.

Education

The civil rights campaigns of the 1950s and 1960s achieved some major legal victories in the field of education (see also Chapters 5 and 6). The 1950 case *Sweatt v. Painter* had established that black and white people were entitled to equal educational resources. The 1954 case *Brown v. Board of Education of Topeka* went further, establishing that a segregated education could never be an equal education. *Brown II* in 1955 and *Cooper v. Aaron* in 1958 attempted to speed up integration. However, in spite of these legal victories, progress towards desegregation was slow. In 1957, two years after *Brown II*, only 750 out of 6300 school districts in the South had desegregated. Consequently, 97 per cent of black students remained in segregated schools. Indeed, the situation had not improved by 1964. Although the Civil Rights Act of 1964 (see Chapter 9, page 54) gave the government power to force the integration of education, by 1968 58 per cent of black schoolchildren in southern states remained in segregated schools. Nonetheless, President Lyndon B. Johnson's Higher Education Act of 1965 led to a fourfold increase in the number of black students attending college and university during the late 1960s and early 1970s (see Chapter 9, page 54).

Transport

The NAACP's case *Morgan v. Virginia* in 1946 (see Chapter 4, page 25) had successfully established that the segregation of interstate transport was illegal. However, CORE's 1961 Freedom Rides (see Chapter 6, page 39) were necessary before the government enforced the desegregation of interstate transport. By September 1961, all of the signs enforcing segregation were removed from interstate buses and bus terminals.

The Montgomery bus boycott of 1955–1956 and the related 1956 court case *Browder v. Gayle* (see Chapter 6, page 36) led to the desegregation of transport in Montgomery. *Browder v. Gayle* also established that the segregation of transport was illegal. However, *de facto* change across the South was slow to follow. Once again, the Civil Rights Act of 1964 was necessary to give the federal government power to enforce desegregation of transport in the South.

Two students in Fort Myer Elementary School, Virginia, face each other on the first day of desegregation, September 1954.

Public places

The sit-ins that began in Greensboro in 1960 (see Chapter 6, page 38) proved to be an effective method for challenging the segregation of public places. By the end of 1963, sit-ins had occurred in 200 cities, as a result of which 161 had desegregated restaurants and canteens. However, local authorities often took measures to avoid rather than enforce desegregation. For example, the authorities in Albany closed public parks and even removed chairs from libraries rather than desegregate. Similarly, even after the Birmingham Campaign of 1963 (see Chapter 7, pages 41–43), the protestors did not achieve the general desegregation of public places within the city. In the year 1964–1965 the Civil Rights Act was used to force a further 53 cities to desegregate. As a result, a total of 214 southern cities had desegregated by the end of 1965.

Voting rights

Eisenhower's Civil Rights Acts of 1957 and 1960 were largely ineffective in guaranteeing black voting rights. Consequently, as late as 1963, only 800,000 of the South's 20 million black citizens were registered to vote.

The Voting Rights Act of 1965 was more effective in increasing voter registration. Between 1965 and 1966 a further 230,000 black people registered to vote across the South. Nonetheless, by 1966 four of the southern states still had fewer than 50 per cent of their black citizens registered to vote. The Voting Rights Act was more effective in the North. In total, the number of black voters in America jumped from four million in 1960 to six million in 1965. Indeed, voter registration led to an increase in the number of black people elected to governmental positions in the North. For example, Robert C. Henry became the first African American to be elected mayor of an American city, becoming Mayor of Springfield, Ohio, in 1966. In 1967, Richard G. Hatcher was elected Mayor of Gary, Indiana, and Carl B. Stokes was elected Mayor of Cleveland, Ohio.

Employment and income

In terms of the levels of employment and income of black Americans, there was a definite improvement during the 1960s but full equality with white Americans was not achieved. Popular pressure on state governments resulted in 25 of the 31 states with the highest proportion of black people introducing Fair Employment Practice laws. In addition, the federal government under Kennedy attempted to ensure fair employment practices for government jobs and for jobs with companies working for the government (see Chapter 9, page 53). Nonetheless, during the 1950s and early 1960s, black unemployment was approximately twice the national average.

The Civil Rights Act of 1964 explicitly outlawed racial discrimination in the job market. Nonetheless, the 1965 the Moynihan Report (see Chapter 8, page 47) highlighted the fact that the income of black workers was only 53 per cent of the national average income. Things had improved by 1968: although black unemployment was 7 per cent and white unemployment was 5 per cent, clearly the gap had closed. Finally, while the average income of black workers had risen by 1968, it was still only 61 per cent of the income of white workers.

Housing

The American census of 1960 reported that 46 per cent of America's black population were living in 'unsound' accommodation. The 1960 census also revealed that 73 per cent of America's black population lived in urban areas where housing stock was old and where the amount of suitable housing available was decreasing. Finally, the census showed that 25 per cent of America's black population lived in inner-city areas in the USA's ten largest cities. These people were living in almost exclusively black areas due to the phenomenon of 'white flight'.

Black campaigners put pressure on American politicians to try and solve these problems. By 1967, 22 states and eight cities had some form of fair housing law. New York State and Massachusetts had comprehensive enforcement agencies dedicated to challenging discrimination in the housing market. However, the majority of these fair housing laws were largely symbolic.

The 1968 Fair Housing Act prohibited discrimination in 80 per cent of America's housing market. However, Congress had toned down the Act and refused to set up an enforcement agency. Additionally, the maximum fine for racial discrimination in the housing market was a mere $1000. Consequently, the Act was an ineffective deterrent to racism in the housing market.

Public support for civil rights

The civil rights campaigns of the early 1960s were highly effective in winning public support. For example, in 1954 55 per cent of those surveyed supported the Supreme Court's decision to make segregation in education illegal. By 1964 80 per cent of the public supported the desegregation of education.

Taking it further

In this chapter we have used statistics to illustrate the extent of the change in America. What are the advantages and disadvantages of statistical data as a historical source for understanding the achievements of the civil rights movement? What would be the advantages and disadvantages of using personal recollections instead?

The Voices of Civil Rights project aims to collect and preserve personal accounts of the civil rights movement in America. Visit their website (www. voicesofcivilrights.org) and read some of the recollections stored there. This may help you to analyse the strengths and weaknesses of this form of information.

However, while white opinion was moving in favour of black rights in theory, many white people still did not want to live near black people. Opinion polls from 1963 show that while 80 per cent of people supported equal rights in terms of employment and voting, only 50 per cent supported equal rights in housing.

Conclusion

The civil rights movement transformed America; by 1968 there had been a legal revolution. Segregation, where it still remained, was no longer backed by the law. What is more, the federal government had new powers to challenge racial injustice. However, *de facto* change was not so comprehensive. Undoubtedly, the USA was a fairer society, but there was still a long way to go before all Americans could be considered 'equal'.

Activity: Helping or hindering?

Examination questions will often ask you to evaluate 'how far…' a state had been reached. For example, you could be asked the question 'How far had racial equality been achieved in America by 1968?' The following activity will prepare you to answer this question.

1. Copy the small cards in the margin.

2. Copy the following spectrum onto a large piece of paper:

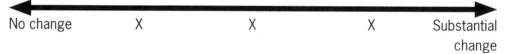

No change   X   X   X   Substantial change

3. Make a list of words that can be used to describe the extent of a change – on the spectrum you have the example 'substantial change'. Choose words from your list to replace the X symbols on your spectrum.

4. Now take the card labelled 'Education *De jure* change'. Using the information in the 'Education' section of this chapter, reach a judgement about how far legal change had been achieved in education. Position the card in the appropriate place on your spectrum. Next to the card, write three bullet-points explaining your decision.

5. Take the card labelled 'Education *De facto* change'. Repeat stage 4, this time assessing how far actual change has been achieved.

6. Repeat the task with the remaining small cards.

7. Choose two of the categories you have studied. For each, write a paragraph explaining how far racial equality had been achieved in that area. Remember to differentiate between *de jure* and *de facto* change. Also, try to use appropriate words to describe the extent of the change.

Education *De facto* change	Education *De jure* change
Transport *De facto* change	Transport *De jure* change
Desegregation of public places *De facto* change	Desegregation of public places *De jure* change
Voting rights *De facto* change	Voting rights *De jure* change
Employment and income *De facto* change	Employment and income *De jure* change
Housing *De facto* change	Housing *De jure* change

Chapter 12 **Reasons for change?**

Key questions

- How far were the American Presidents responsible for dismantling segregation in the South?
- How far was Martin Luther King responsible for the successes of the civil rights movement between 1955 and 1968?
- What role did grassroots activists and America's black citizens play in the successes of the civil rights movement between 1955 and 1968?

Between 1945 and 1968 America witnessed a civil rights revolution. But who was responsible? Was it the civil rights leaders, America's Presidents or the activists themselves? In 1938 the black intellectual C.L.R. James asked a similar question about the Haitian revolution, a slave revolt that led to the establishment of the first black republic outside of Africa. James's answer is contained in the book *Black Jacobins* (1938), a work that marked the beginning of black history as it is currently understood. James argues that the ordinary black people of Haiti made their revolution. To what extent was the same true in America?

Take note

As you read this chapter complete the following table.

Factor	How far were they responsible for change?	Limit of their influence on change
The Presidents		
Civil rights leaders		
Peaceful protest and mass activism		

The Presidents

Certainly, American Presidents played a role in advancing racial justice. However, for Eisenhower, and to some extent Kennedy, it was a role they played reluctantly. The Little Rock Campaign and the Freedom Rides show that both men needed to be pushed to act by civil rights activists. Johnson was much more proactive. He used his influence in the Senate to ensure that the Civil Rights Acts of 1957 and the 1960s became law. Nonetheless, he too followed the campaigners. The impetus behind the 1965 Voting Rights Act, for example, came from the voter registration campaigns, such as the Mississippi Freedom Summer, organised by the Student Nonviolent Coordinating Committee (SNCC) and Congress of Racial Equality (CORE) in 1964. In general the Presidents played an important role in convincing Congress to act, but it was the civil rights campaigns and not the Presidents that kept the issue of racial justice on the political agenda.

Martin Luther King

King undoubtedly played a major role in the campaign. King's great strength was his ability to inspire. He was highly charismatic and a gifted orator who could convey the injustices of segregation to a national audience. In this sense he was an ideal spokesperson for black Christians in the southern states. As a result he was a good leader for the television age. Indeed, his campaigns and speeches were responsible for swinging public support behind the civil rights legislation of the mid-1960s.

Nonetheless, he was also a divisive figure. Conservatives criticised him for taking protest to the street. In a democracy, they argued, campaigners should work through the courts and through Congress. He was also criticised for using children in his campaigns. Radicals, on the other hand, thought that King was too cautious. They criticised him for being too close to white politicians. For example, he was criticised for rerouting a march during the Albany campaign of 1961 at President Johnson's request. Young activists were also worried that King was trying to dominate the campaign. SNCC leaders, for example, felt that he wanted to make SNCC a subsection of the Southern Christian Leadership Conference (SCLC).

King was also criticised following the Chicago campaign of 1966 for misunderstanding the situation in the North. Local leaders claimed that he had not appreciated the scale of the problem nor proposed a workable solution to the problems of Chicago. Similarly, many, even within the SCLC, believed that the Poor People's Campaign of 1968 was impractical and poorly focused. King was unable to unite the northern black working class, many of whom did not share his Christian faith. Finally, following 1965, King's charisma and oratory failed to persuade the public of the need to tackle poverty or the problems of ghettoisation.

Peaceful protest and mass activism

Behind the leaders of the civil rights movement stood countless activists, campaigners and ordinary black people who put their safety on the line to campaign for freedom. Martin Luther King and James Farmer (see pages 75–6) were important because they spoke for these people. Without a mass following the movement's leaders would have had less authority when speaking to the media and less authority when bargaining with politicians.

The scale of protest during the 1950s and 1960s is staggering. During the Montgomery bus boycott, 85 per cent of Montgomery's black people boycotted the buses. Similarly, 70,000 people took part in the sit-in movement of the early 1960s. Notably, the sit-ins were initially spontaneous and not linked to a specific organisation or leader. The scale of the March on Washington also demonstrated the popular force behind the campaign. Around 250,000 marchers, 80 per cent of whom were black, came together under the slogan 'Free by '63', demonstrating the popular desire for justice.

Peaceful protest was also highly effective in the late 1950s and early 1960s due to the fact that it attracted media attention. Television pictures of police brutality against unarmed peaceful protestors did much to persuade the American public that segregation should end. However, the campaigns in Albany and Chicago showed that the method did not guarantee success.

Conclusion

The combination of mass action and skilful leadership kept racial justice on the political agenda, forcing reluctant politicians to deliver legal change. The Presidents, too, had a role to play in managing Congress and persuading its members to embrace change.

Taking it further

This chapter has discussed a series of individuals who played a part in the civil rights victories of the 1960s. Nonetheless, this list is by no means complete. Look back over your notes from the earlier chapters in this Section and make a list of the other people who made a contribution to the campaign. For example, E.D. Nixon (see Chapter 6), and Jesse Jackson (see Chapter 8) all played a role in the campaign. Make flash cards for all of these figures noting their contribution to the civil rights campaigns.

Activity: Dear Mr James

Reread the 'hook' to this chapter.

Write a letter to C.L.R. James explaining how far you agree that the black people of America were responsible for the end of segregation in the southern states.

Skills Builder 2: Planning answers to questions on causation and change

Questions on causation

In the AS examination you may be asked questions on causation – questions about what caused historical events to take place.

Some questions may ask you to explain why something happened. For example:

> (A) Why was the Civil Rights Act of 1964 passed?

Other questions on causation will ask you to assess the importance of one cause of an event in relation to other causes. These often begin with 'How far' or 'To what extent'. Here is an example:

> (B) How far do you agree that the assassination of President Kennedy was the main reason for the passing of the Civil Rights Act in 1964?

Planning your answer

Before you write your essay you need to make a plan. In the exam you will have to do this very quickly! The first thing to do is to identify the key points you will make in your answer. Let's look at some examples.

When planning an answer to Question (A) you need to note down reasons why the Civil Rights Act of 1964 was passed. You can do this in the form of a list or a mind map.

When planning an answer to Question (B) you need to think about the importance of each reason. You could:

- Write a list of all the reasons then number them in order of importance.

- Draw a mind map with 'The Civil Rights Act of 1964' at the centre and put the most important reasons near the middle and the least important reasons further away.

It is much easier to assess the importance of one factor when you have a list of all relevant factors in front of you!

The information you require for these answers can be found in Chapter 9. Go to Chapter 9 and identify the reasons why the Civil Rights Act was passed. Focus not only on Kennedy's assassination but also on the efforts of civil rights campaigners, President Johnson's skilful management of Congress and public opinion.

Linking the causes

Once you have identified the relevant information and organised it, it is important to highlight links between the reasons.

In making your plan, try grouping reasons together which have links. If you have produced a list of reasons, you may want to rearrange the points where you can identify clear links between them. If you have drawn a mind map, you could draw arrows between the linked points.

Writing your answer

For Question (A) above, you could write a paragraph on each cause. Alternatively, you might want to start with what you think is the most important cause and then deal with the other causes.

For Question (B) above, it is essential that you refer to the relative importance of different causes, focusing particularly on the role of Kennedy's assassination. Remember to answer the question! You might want to deal with Kennedy's assassination first and then assess the importance of other points in the passing of the 1964 Civil Rights Act. Make sure you write a separate paragraph for each reason that you identify.

In your concluding paragraph, make sure that you reach a judgement on 'how far' Kennedy's assassination was the major reason why the Civil Rights Act was passed.

Questions about change

These questions will require you to explain how far a specified factor changed during a historical period. Examples of this type of question would be:

> (C) How far did the methods used by the civil rights campaigners change in the period 1954–1968?

> (D) How far had equality for black Americans been achieved by 1968?

Planning your answer

When you plan, organise your material in a way that will help you to answer the question.

For instance, for Question (C) you could begin by listing two or three ways in which the methods used by the civil rights campaigners changed. Having done that, you could list two or three ways in which the methods stayed the same. Alternatively, you could arrange this information on one or two mind maps. Remember that your answer needs to be balanced. Therefore, it should provide points for and against change. Each of these points will form the basis for one paragraph in your answer. In the last Skills Builder section, you considered the importance of providing specific examples to support your points. Don't forget this!

When you plan, there is no need to organise your material in a chronological way. This may encourage the writing of descriptive or narrative-style answers. Such answers may contain lots of accurate and relevant historical information but may not be directly focused on the question.

Writing your answer

In Questions (C) and (D) you are asked 'how far' in relation to changes. So in your final paragraph – the conclusion – you will be expected to make a judgement. Based on the historical evidence you have presented in your answer, you should decide, and state, whether you believe the situation mainly changed or stayed the same.

Activity: How much have you learned?

Here are some examples of questions which deal with causation and change. First, identify the causation questions and give a reason to support your choice. Then identify the questions which deal with change and give a reason for your choice. Finally, choose one 'causation' question and one 'change' question and produce a plan for each, showing how you would organise your answer.

> (E) How far was the leadership of Martin Luther King responsible for the gains made by the civil rights movement in the years 1955–1968?

> (F) How far do you agree that the Federal Government became more sympathetic to civil rights in the period 1945–1968?

> (G) To what extent were black Americans still facing discrimination in 1968?

> (H) Why was civil and legal equality for black Americans not achieved until 1964–1965?

Chapter 13 Malcolm X – an alternative vision

Key questions

- What were the key teachings of the Nation of Islam?
- How did Malcolm X's vision differ from that of Martin Luther King?
- How did Malcolm X's views change towards the end of his life?

Martin Luther King's dream was Malcolm X's nightmare. Malcolm X was highly critical of the aims, methods and achievements of the civil rights movement. He claimed that the key consequence of civil rights campaigns was that black people could 'sit down next to white folks – on the toilet.' Malcolm X acknowledged that segregation was a form of oppression, but he believed that integration would bring about a new, more subtle, form of enslavement.

Take note

As you read through the section below, complete the following table:

History	Beliefs

Add notes to the table to show links between the development of the Nation of Islam and the development of its beliefs.

Glossary:

Black Power

A political slogan that originated in the United States around which black radicals united. It emphasises racial pride and the creation of black political and cultural organisations in order to ensure black liberation and autonomy.

Introduction

Malcolm X rose to prominence as one of the leading lights of the Nation of Islam, an organisation that had been established in the 1930s and was led by Elijah Muhammad. During this time Malcolm preached a political message that he described as 'Black Nationalism.' Malcolm X's ideas were distinctive and clearly opposed to those of Martin Luther King and led to the rise of **Black Power**.

In the mid 1960s, Malcolm X left the Nation of Islam and redefined his position, establishing the Organization of Afro-American Unity (OAAU). In this final phase of his campaign he began to talk about co-operation with other black civil rights leaders, although he continued to argue that African Americans could only be free if they controlled their own communities.

The Nation of Islam

Foundation and beliefs

The Nation of Islam was founded by **Wallace Fard Muhammad** in 1930. Between 1930 and 1934 Fard outlined a distinctive teaching which became the basis of the organisation. According to Fard, God, whose name in Islam is Allah, created man. The first humans were black, but 6000 years ago the evil scientist Yacub started selective breeding in order to create white people. The white people that Yacub bred were morally weak and unable to do good. However, in the centuries that followed they enslaved all people who were not white. This doctrine, which asserts the superiority of black people, has been called **black supremacism**.

Following Fard's mysterious disappearance in 1934, **Elijah Muhammad** led the Nation of Islam and gave Fard's original teachings a practical and political edge. Muhammad taught that black and white people could not live together in peace. Consequently, he advocated separatism – that is to say, that black people should *choose* to live apart from white people. In practical terms this meant creating a self-governing all-black state in the territory of North America.

Finally, Muhammad's practical message to black people was to stay pure and work hard. Black people could be seduced in northern cities by drugs, cigarettes, alcohol and sex. He taught that these – along with coffee, pork, jazz, blues, gambling and the cinema – were another way of enslaving black people. Purity and hard work were believed to be the only way in which black people could guarantee self-improvement.

The Nation of Islam and black Americans

The Nation of Islam was particularly attractive to young black men in the working-class areas of northern cities. Many were trying to escape from the glamorous but largely illegal world of gambling, prostitution and drugs. The Nation of Islam encouraged black men to find dignity in hard work and self-discipline. This message was especially appealing to black ex-convicts. Indeed, 90 per cent of members of New York's **Temple Number Seven** had criminal records. Significantly, practically none of the ex-convicts who joined the Nation of Islam re-offended. The Nation of Islam's message to black men to 'clean yourself up, stand up and do something for yourself' proved inspirational.

Malcolm X's background

An awareness of Malcolm X's life and experiences is essential to understanding his political views. He has been accused of being a racist, but it would be wrong to dismiss his message. Indeed, his ideas should be understood as a response to the white supremacist society in which he was raised.

Early life

Whereas Martin Luther King had a relatively privileged middle-class upbringing, Malcolm X's early life was extremely disadvantaged. His family was no stranger to racist violence; his father was active in Negro organisations and his mother was of mixed race. Indeed, three of Malcolm's uncles were murdered by whites. Furthermore, the Black Legion, a white supremacist organisation similar to the Ku Klux Klan, torched his father's home. There is also evidence that the Black Legion murdered his father – although the Milwaukee police claimed that the death was an accident.

Earl Little, Malcolm X's father, died when Malcolm was only six years old, plunging the family into poverty. Shortly after his father's death his mother, Louise Little, suffered from a nervous breakdown and her children were sent to foster homes. In spite of these turbulent early experiences, Malcolm X proved to be an excellent student. However, he dropped out of school after a teacher told him that his desire to become a lawyer was 'no realistic goal for a nigger.'

Wallace Fard Muhammad

The founder of the Nation of Islam. Little is known for certain about Muhammad, but all agree that he disappeared in 1934 in mysterious circumstances.

Elijah Muhammad

(1897–1975)

The second leader of the Nation of Islam, responsible for establishing it as a mass movement in the 1940s and 1950s.

Glossary:

Black supremacism

The belief that black people are superior to white people.

Temple Number Seven

A meeting place for followers of the Nation of Islam in Harlem, New York.

Take note

Draw a timeline mapping out the important events in Malcolm X's life. Start with his birth in 1925.

Source 13.1: A New York taxi driver gives his views on Malcolm X in 1961

I dig Malcolm the best. He's the only one that makes any sense for my money. I'm too busy making a buck to join a movement. But those black Muslims, whatever you call them, make more sense than the NAACP and all the rest of them put together. They're for their own people and that Malcolm ain't afraid to tell the FBI or the cops where to get off. You don't see him pussyfootin' around the whites like he's scared of them.

Taken from: *Black Power* by Jeffrey Ogbonna Green Ogbar (2005)

Take note

As you work through this section, make a spider diagram of Malcolm X's beliefs like the one below.

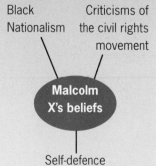

Black Nationalism   Criticisms of the civil rights movement

Malcolm X's beliefs

Self-defence

Draw lines between the different aspects of Malcolm X's thoughts to show the way his ideas link together. For example, you could link the importance of self-defence to his criticisms of Martin Luther King's pacifism.

As a young man Malcolm X moved to New York. After a series of low-paid jobs, he become involved in New York's criminal underworld. In 1946, as a result of his criminal activities, he was sentenced to 10 years in prison.

Conversion and the Nation of Islam

Malcolm X used his time in prison to further his education. It was also during this time that he came into contact with the Nation of Islam. The Nation of Islam's message deeply affected Malcolm X. His lifestyle and behaviour changed dramatically; he became highly self-disciplined and gave up smoking. The Nation of Islam's focus on the shared African heritage of black Americans also inspired Malcolm X to change his name from Malcolm Little to Malcolm X. He rejected 'Little' as it was the name given to his family by a white slave owner; he adopted X as a symbol that his real African name had been lost.

Following his release from prison in 1952, Malcolm X gained significant influence within the Nation of Islam. His ability to relate to working-class black men and his powerful oratory attracted many new converts. Indeed, between 1952 and 1953, thanks largely to Malcolm X, membership of the Detroit Temple tripled. As a result, Muhammad gave him more responsibility, and between 1957 and 1959 the number of temples shot up from 27 to 49.

White reporters in the American media were shocked by the growth of the Nation of Islam. In 1959, CBS journalist Mike Wallace made a documentary entitled *The Hate that Hate Produced*. The documentary was intended to portray the Nation of Islam as a sinister organisation. However, an extended interview with Malcolm X convinced many urban blacks that the Nation of Islam represented their hopes and desires. In the two months after the documentary was broadcast, national membership of the Nation of Islam doubled.

Malcolm X's beliefs

Criticisms of the civil rights movement

Twentieth-century Uncle Tom

Malcolm X was highly critical of both Martin Luther King – calling him the 'twentieth-century **Uncle Tom**' – and the civil rights movement more generally. Essentially, he argued that organisations like the Southern Christian Leadership Conference (SCLC) and the National Association for the Advancement of Colored People (NAACP) were taken in by American myths like the American dream. They trusted the American system and therefore they would never be able to set black people free.

What is more, Malcolm X openly claimed that Martin Luther King was being paid by the white government to preach Christian love and forgiveness, and in so doing he was preventing black people from effectively fighting for their rights. Malcolm X's criticisms of the March on Washington of August 1963 are a good example; he described it as 'nothing but a circus with clowns and all' organised by a bunch of 'Uncle Toms' who were slavishly serving their white masters.

New forms of slavery

Malcolm X was also critical of Martin Luther King's goals. Integration, he argued, would bring in a new form of slavery. His view was that integration in the North had led to the creation of an underclass of black people who were addicted to drugs and who wasted their money on gambling, alcohol and prostitution. These vices, he claimed, were deliberately introduced to trap black people and prevent them from improving their lives.

Black Nationalism

Whereas Martin Luther King pointed to America's national tradition of democracy and respect for individual rights and demanded that this be fully extended to African Americans, Malcolm X described himself as a '*Black Nationalist* Freedom Fighter'. He argued that the American nation had been founded on the principles of white supremacy. As a result he rejected American values and refused to call himself an American.

> **Glossary:**
> **'Uncle Tom'**
>
> A term of abuse applied to black people who do not stand up for their rights and have a slavish attitude towards white people. It is a reference to a fictional character in Harriet Beecher Stowe's novel *Uncle Tom's Cabin* (1852).

> **Source 13.2: Malcolm X speaking in his 'The Ballot or the Bullet' speech, 1964**
>
> And when I speak, I don't speak as a Democrat, or a Republican, nor an American. I speak as a victim of America's so-called democracy. You and I have never seen democracy; all we've seen is hypocrisy. When we open our eyes today and look around America, we see America not through the eyes of someone who... has enjoyed the fruits of Americanism, we see America through the eyes of someone who has been the victim of Americanism. We don't see any American dream; we've experienced only the American nightmare. We haven't benefited from America's democracy; we've only suffered from America's hypocrisy. And the generation that's coming up now can see it and are not afraid to say it.
>
> Extract from: American Rhetoric Top 100 Speeches (http://www.americanrhetoric.com)

Malcolm X's alternative to American nationalism was Black Nationalism. By this Malcolm X meant two things:

- *Political Black Nationalism* meant self-determination, that is to say black people should govern themselves.
- *Economic Black Nationalism* meant that black people should control the economy within their community.

Malcolm X argued that Black Nationalism was only possible in a black community that excluded white people.

> **Source 13.3: Malcolm X describes Black Nationalism in his 'The Ballot or the Bullet' speech, 1964**
>
> I don't believe in fighting today in any one front, but on all fronts. In fact, I'm a 'Black Nationalist Freedom Fighter'... So today, though Islam is my religious philosophy, my political, economic, and social philosophy is Black Nationalism... The political philosophy of Black Nationalism only means that the black man should control the politics and the politicians in his own community... The time when white people can come in our community and get us to vote for them so that they can be our political leaders and tell us what to do and what not to do is long gone... The economic philosophy of Black Nationalism only means that we should own and operate and control the economy of our community.
>
> Extract from: American Rhetoric Top 100 Speeches (http://www.americanrhetoric.com)

Self-defence

Malcolm X's emphasis on self-defence was in clear contrast to King's message of nonviolence. Malcolm X believed that King's strategy re-emphasised that

Malcolm X speaking at a rally, June 1963.

stereotype of the weak and defenceless black person. He argued that white racists – in his eyes, this included the American government – did not respect peaceful protest. In this way, he claimed that peaceful protest could not bring about substantial change. Additionally, he argued that it was impossible for any sane person to love people who had beaten or raped them, or who had killed one of their friends.

Malcolm X believed that self-defence was a more powerful weapon than love and forgiveness. He advocated gun ownership on the part of black Americans, and claimed that using violence in self-defence was a natural and empowering response to hatred. Famously, he said that black Americans should liberate themselves 'by all means necessary.'

Break with the Nation of Islam

Malcolm X's fame soured his relationship with Elijah Muhammad. Muhammad was jealous of the attention that Malcolm X received. What is more, on occasions Malcolm X's statements embarrassed the Nation of Islam. For example, in 1963, Malcolm X described President Kennedy's assassination as 'chickens coming home to roost', implying that Kennedy had got what he deserved. As a result of these tensions, Malcolm X left the Nation of Islam in March 1964.

Organisation of Afro-American Unity

Following his break from the Nation of Islam, Malcolm X set up a new group, the Organization of Afro-American Unity (OAAU). The OAAU drew a link between the struggle against white oppression in America and the **anti-colonial struggle in Africa**. It aimed to organise and **re-educate** black Americans in order to gain economic security for black people across the world. In America, the OAAU organised:

- voter registration campaigns
- school boycotts in areas where the education for black people was unsatisfactory
- rent strikes where housing was inadequate
- social programmes to help drug addicts.

In addition, the OAAU encouraged re-education through publishing new textbooks and developing new teaching methods, including home schooling, to emphasise self-reliance, black pride and solidarity with black Africans struggling against colonialism.

Integration

In his final year, Malcolm X also began to rethink the possibility of integration. First, in his 1964 speech 'The Ballot or the Bullet', he advocated working within the American political system. He argued that black people could use their voting power to elect black politicians.

Second, he announced his willingness to work with organisations such as the

Congress of Racial Equality (CORE) and Student Nonviolent Coordinating Committee (SNCC) in order to improve conditions for black people. Indeed, there was even discussion of co-operation between Malcolm X and Martin Luther King.

Finally, after his **Hajj**, Malcolm X began to reconsider the possibility of a society in which black and white people could live side by side as equals. Whilst in Mecca he witnessed true harmony between black and white Muslims. Similarly, during his visit to Africa he saw white students who were genuinely helping to improve conditions for black people. Both of these experiences led him to embrace the possibility that racial harmony could exist in America.

Assassination

Following Malcolm X's break with the Nation of Islam, the FBI received reports that Muhammad had ordered his assassination. Indeed, there were numerous attempts on his life throughout 1964, including a firebomb that destroyed his family home. Finally, in February 1965 Malcolm X was shot 15 times at close range. The three men convicted of his murder were all members of the Nation of Islam.

> **Source 13.4: British Civil Rights Campaigner and journalist Darcus Howe recalls meeting Malcolm X during his visit to Trinidad**
>
> I have never seen such a remarkable personality in my life. I've met prime ministers, I've met presidents, I've spoken to Nelson Mandela. He was clear in his bearing and his certainty of language – one of the finest political leaders of all time.
> Taken from Channel 4 website

Conclusion

Malcolm X's significance was his ability to express the feelings of America's black working class. Following Malcolm X's assassination, the Organization of Afro-American Unity collapsed, but many of its aims became central to other radical groups, particularly SNCC and the Black Panther Party.

Activity: Role Play – imaginary meeting

Martin Luther King and Malcolm X only ever met once, and then only briefly. Using your notes from this chapter on Malcolm X and your notes from previous chapters on Martin Luther King, prepare a five-minute script of an imaginary meeting between these two historical figures. At their meeting they should explain their views, discuss their differences and criticise each other. Their political beliefs are linked to their personal experiences so make sure you bring in relevant examples from their life stories in the discussion.

Glossary:

Hajj

A pilgrimage to Mecca, Islam's holiest city. Muslims are expected to make this journey at least once in their lives.

Taking it further

You can find audio and text files of Malcolm X's *Ballot or the Bullet* speech in the Internet. Find a complete version of the speech and then imagine that you have been asked to produce a news report about it. You must include a summary of the speech, an explanation of its significance, and extracts from it to illustrate your points.

Chapter 14 Creative tension? Divisions in the civil rights movement

Key questions

- What were the major sources of tension in the civil rights movement?
- What were the effects of the tensions in the civil rights movement during the late 1960s?

Following the passing of the 1965 Voting Rights Act, President Johnson expected racial tensions to ease. However, less than a week after the passing of the Act, the Watts neighbourhood of Los Angeles was engulfed by unprecedented violence during a six-day race riot that destroyed entire buildings and claimed 34 lives. The riots reflected the fact that Johnson's civil rights legislation had done nothing to stamp out police racism or poverty in urban ghettos. At the same time tensions in the civil rights coalition came to a head, undermining the unity that had led to the dramatic gains of the early 1960s.

Take note

As you read through this section make notes in the form of a spider diagram as suggested below.

Timeline

1965	Watts Riots in Los Angeles
1966	Shooting of James Meredith James Farmer resigns as leader of CORE SNCC embraces self-defence and expels white members NAACP and NUL walk out of negotiations with SCLC and SNCC
1968	SNCC embrace the use of 'revolutionary violence' CORE expels white members

Tensions at the heart of the civil rights movement

From the very beginning there were divisions within the civil rights movement. These divisions arose from disagreements over methods and the goals for which black Americans were fighting. There were also personality clashes, not to mention jealousy and rivalry, between the leaders who were competing for media attention and public recognition.

During the 1960s the American media presented some groups as radical and others as moderate. The National Association for the Advancement of Colored People (NAACP) and the National Urban League (NUL), for example, were presented as moderates due to their commitment to work through the courts and their willingness to work with America's white population. On the other hand, from the mid-1960s, the Congress of Racial Equality (CORE) and the Student Nonviolent Coordinating Committee (SNCC) were called radicals because they advocated self-defence. In addition, Martin Luther King and the Southern Christian Leadership Conference (SCLC) were criticised by the moderates for being too radical, while the radicals attacked them for being too moderate.

Labels such as 'radical' or 'moderate' were not entirely fixed. The aims and methods of groups changed over time, and so did the labels applied to them. Notably, SNCC, CORE and the SCLC all became more radical during the 1960s.

Sources of tension

Ideological splits within the civil rights movement focused on four major issues:

- the use of violence in the fight for black civil rights
- the extent to which black and white people should collaborate in the campaign for racial equality
- how far *de jure* change could bring about *de facto* change
- the extent to which black people should seek integration.

Methods

Peaceful methods or violent protest?

In the late 1950s and the early 1960s, King and the SCLC proved the effectiveness of peaceful direct action as a weapon for challenging segregation. King's commitment to nonviolence was based on his heartfelt belief in Christianity and Jesus' teaching that Christians should 'turn the other cheek'.

SNCC and CORE also organised campaigns using peaceful protest. Their commitment to peaceful methods was pragmatic rather than ideological. They used these methods because they worked. Additionally, they believed that nonviolent tactics were compatible with self-defence. For example, some SNCC activists in the South were willing to accept protection from black farmers armed with guns. Radicals were critical of nonviolent protest and disagreed with the principle on which it was based. Malcolm X, for example, argued that black people should be prepared to use any means to fight white oppression.

In 1966 the shooting of James Meredith (see Chapter 6, page 40) prompted SNCC to emphasise its commitment to self-defence. In 1962 Meredith was the first black student to be admitted to the University of Mississippi. He was shot and injured on his March Against Fear, a march through the state of Mississippi to encourage voter registration there. **Stokely Carmichael** argued that Meredith's shooting underlined the need for black people to use violence to defend themselves. SNCC became even more radical in 1968 as Carmichael proposed using revolutionary violence against the US government. CORE also moved away from non-violence during the late 1960s, prompting the resignation of CORE's leader **James Farmer** in 1966.

Collaboration?

The civil rights movement was also split over the question of how far black people should collaborate with white people in the fight against racism. The NAACP and SCLC, for example, welcomed black and white members, arguing that co-operation would make the movement stronger. Radicals, on the other

Martin Luther King and Stokely Carmichael walk together on the March Against Fear in Philadelphia, June 1966.

Stokely Carmichael

(1941–1998)

Trinidad-born leader of the Student Nonviolent Coordinating Committee (SNCC) from 1966. He was involved in the Freedom Rides of 1961 and subsequently became a member of SNCC. His radical position on many issues made him a natural ally of the Black Panthers. He was appointed Prime Minister of the Black Panthers in the 1970s.

James Farmer

(1920–1999)

Leader of the Congress of Racial Equality (CORE) from 1942. He was a leading figure in CORE's Freedom Rides of 1961. He spoke at the March on Washington in 1963. However, he resigned from the CORE leadership in 1966 due to CORE's increasing radicalisation.

Source 14.1: Stokely Carmichael speaks to members of the SNCC in 1966

Too often the goal 'integration' has been based on a complete acceptance of the fact that in order to have a decent house or education, Negros must move into a white neighbourhood. This reinforces the idea that 'white' is automatically better and that 'black' is by definition inferior. It allows the nation to focus on a handful of Negro children who get into white schools, and to ignore the 94 per cent who are left behind. Such situations will not change until Negros have political power – to control their own schools.

Taken from: *Black Power* by Jeffrey Ogbonna Green Ogbar (2005)

hand, saw dangers in collaborative working. Black people, they argued, should liberate themselves. Others went further, suggesting that white people simply could not understand the experience of black people or the problems that they faced. As a result they rejected biracial co-operation.

SNCC and CORE moved away from mixed membership in the late 1960s. For example, in 1966 SNCC expelled all white members. Similarly, in 1965 CORE decided that black people must form the majority of the organisation, and in 1968 whites were officially excluded from membership.

Using the law?

There were also disagreements regarding the effectiveness of legal change. The NAACP, NUL and SCLC all fought for legal change. In this sense they were committed to working within the American legal system. However, the absence of legal segregation in the northern states meant that northern blacks gained little from their legal victories. Consequently, SNCC and CORE began to focus on the economic and political issues faced by black citizens in northern ghettos.

Goals of the civil rights movement

Integration?

Racial integration was at the heart of the campaigns of groups such as the NACCP and the SCLC. The case of *Brown v. the Board of Education* (1954), for example, aimed to force white schools to accept black students. Initially, SNCC and CORE fought for the same cause in campaigns such as the Greensboro sit-ins and the Freedom Rides.

However, in the mid-1960s, SNCC's Stokely Carmichael began to stress the importance of black control over public services rather than integration. Carmichael's argument was twofold: first he stated that traditional integrationist campaigns such as the Brown case only changed education for a handful of black students while the majority stayed in underfunded colleges. To address this problem, he then argued that black people should campaign for control over local schools in order to ensure a high standard of education for black students.

Separatism?

The Nation of Islam went further still. During the 1950s, Malcolm X argued that white people would never stop trying to enslave black people. Consequently, black freedom was only possible in an all-black society. For this reason Malcolm X rejected integration in favour of separatism – black people living and working in exclusive black communities that they controlled.

Personalities

The divisions within the civil rights movement were personal as well as political. King became the focus of a great deal of criticism from other groups who believed that he dominated the movement; that he was essentially a glory seeker who used the campaigns to make a name for himself and that he was controlled by the white government.

SNCC and CORE were also critical of King. They accused him of treating them as junior partners in the civil rights movement. For example, King suggested that the SNCC should become the 'student wing' of SCLC. SNCC, however, were keen to remain independent. CORE, on the other hand, felt that King was not supportive of their campaigns. For example, they criticised him for not playing a more prominent role in the Freedom Rides of 1961.

Civil rights leaders were keen for media attention and competed with each other for the media spotlight. Notably, there were criticisms that King dominated media attention. CORE's James Farmer was determined to use the Freedom Rides to gain attention for CORE, and SNCC used their Freedom Summer campaign in a similar way. Competition was fierce because all of the leaders knew that the media attention was essential to raise funds and increase the membership of their organisations.

Similarly, SNCC and CORE activists were concerned that King was working too closely with Presidents Kennedy and Johnson. Radicals objected to working with the government because they felt that it had failed to protect protestors during the civil rights campaigns.

Personal relationships reached a low point in 1966 during negotiations between the NAACP, SCLC, CORE, SNCC and the NUL over a protest march following the shooting of James Meredith. Carmichael, SNCC's leader, argued that he would no longer work with NAACP and NUL due to their conservatism and their willingness to work with white lawyers and politicians. The leaders of the NAACP and the NUL walked out after Carmichael showered them with verbal abuse.

Vietnam

Black activists were also divided on the Vietnam War. Leaders of the NAACP supported the war. They believed that any criticism would drive a wedge between civil rights campaigners and the government, and therefore slow down progress towards racial justice.

Radicals in SNCC, however, believed that the Vietnam War was a racial war between the white American government and the Asian people of Vietnam. Therefore, they were highly critical of the war. King initially refused to criticise the campaign. As a result, SNCC and other radical groups publicly criticised him. However, as time went on King felt a moral obligation to speak out against the war as it violated his commitment to peace. His public rejection of the war heightened tensions between King and the NAACP.

Effects of the tension

Creative tensions

The tensions between the different civil rights groups had some very positive effects. **Whitney Young** of the National Urban League (NUL), for example, claimed that it was possible for experienced campaigners to use the tensions to their advantage. Young argued that every time Malcolm X or Carmichael criticised the NUL it became easier to work with white politicians and

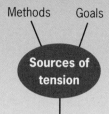

business leaders. These criticisms persuaded white leaders that the NUL was a respectable organisation because the criticisms implied that NUL was moderate and that there were significant differences between the NUL and groups like SNCC, whose radicalism increasingly frightened the white establishment. Equally, Young claimed that in spite of their differences he had a good relationship with Malcolm X. Indeed, whenever the NUL were having difficult negotiations, Young would ask Malcolm X to telephone the obstinate employers. One call from Malcolm X was usually enough to scare the employers into talking to the NUL.

Destructive tensions

Tensions also had a negative impact on the fight for black freedom. First, they damaged King's reputation and showed that he was not really the spokesman for every black citizen in America. King's weakness was obvious during the Watts riots, when the crowds ignored his plea for an end to the violence. Second, following 1966, groups such as SNCC and CORE were no longer prepared to work with the NAACP, the SCLC or NUL, and the fragmentation of the movement meant that it was difficult to organise national campaigns.

Conclusion

The apparent unity of the civil rights movement in the early 1960s was a façade concealing personal rivalries and political disagreements. The breakdown of the civil rights coalition was due to the radicalism of CORE and SNCC, the growing influence of Malcolm X, the culture of the northern ghettos, and the fact that government authorities were becoming increasingly adept at dealing with nonviolent protest.

Activity: One big essay

Taking it further

The 'One big essay' activity considers a *why* question. How would you reorganise your essay if you were dealing with a *how far* question? Try to answer the following question:
'How far were personal differences the main cause of fragmentation in the civil rights movement following 1966?'

1. As a class, divide into five groups. Each group should be allocated one of the following factors that contributed to divisions in the civil rights movement:

   - peace or violence
   - collaboration with whites
   - legal campaigns
   - separatism or integration
   - personalities.

2. Each group should write a paragraph that explains how this factor led to a split in the movement. They should address the question: 'Why did the civil rights movement become fragmented after 1966?' Each paragraph should: begin with a direct answer to the question; contain three specific examples that support the point that is being made; conclude with a sentence that explains why the factor led to greater fragmentation.

3. Each paragraph should be assessed using the three criteria given above.

Chapter 15   **Power to the people! The Black Panthers**

Key questions

- What were the aims of the Black Panthers?
- How did the Black Panthers' initiative seek to achieve their aims?
- Who opposed the Black Panthers and why?

Bobby Hutton, also known as Lil' Bobby, was the youngest member of the Black Panthers. He joined the Party in 1966 at the age of 16. He died two years later in 'the battle of 28th Street', a firefight with the Oakland police.

The battle started when eight Panthers ambushed a group of police, in response to the assassination of Martin Luther King. Hutton and another of the Panthers fled, escaping arrest. The Oakland police sent a 50-man assault squad to capture them. The police fired on the building where Hutton was hiding for over an hour and threw tear gas canisters into the house, forcing the two men to surrender. Unarmed, Hutton walked out of the house with his hands up, but the police shot him 12 times, killing him instantly. What was it about the Black Panthers that led the police to respond in this way?

Timeline

1961	*The Wretched of the Earth* published
1966	Black Panther party (BPP) founded Ten-Point Programme published BPP launches 'Patrol the Pigs' campaign
1967	Huey P. Newton arrested for murder BPP launches the 'Free Huey' campaign
1968	BPP launch survival programmes Eldridge Cleaver stands as Presidential Candidate for the Peace and Freedom Party 'Chicago Seven' arrested Eldridge Cleaver's *Soul on Ice* published
1977	BPP disbanded

Origins and aims of the Black Panthers

The Black Panther Party (BPP) was founded on 15 October 1966 by **Huey P. Newton** and **Bobby Seale**. The Party was one of the most radical organisations formed during the struggle for black rights in the 1960s. Its membership was all-black, it was prepared to use violence and its aim was the revolutionary transformation of America.

Huey P. Newton

(1942–1989)

Co-founder of the BPP. He grew up in a working-class family and was largely educated outside of the school system. In the 1970s he went to university; he gained a PhD in 1980. During this time he published a number of academic pieces. He was murdered in 1989 by a drug dealer.

Bobby Seale

(born 1936)

Co-founder of the BPP. He was born in Texas and therefore had early experience of segregation. He moved to Oakland, California, in 1962. He was arrested with the Chicago Seven but was tried separately. The judge ordered that he should be bound and gagged during the trial, due to his interruptions. In later life he co-authored a recipe book entitled *Barbequing with Bobby* and went on to become a spokesman for Ben & Jerry's ice cream.

Glossary:
Militia

A military force made up of ordinary people rather than professional soldiers.

Take note

Make a three-column table. In the first column, summarise the ten demands set out in the Ten-Point Programme (see Source 15.1). You will complete the second and third columns of the table as you read through the chapter.

Seale and Newton had been involved in campaigns for black rights since the early 1960s. Both looked to Malcolm X as a role model. They admired Malcolm X's ability to communicate with the black working class who lived in the ghettos of the North. Newton publicly stated 'the Black Panther Party exists in the spirit of Malcolm.' Like Malcolm X, Newton and Seale were critical of the civil rights leadership who chose to work with white people for being too cautious and failing to understand the needs of the black working class.

Newton and Seale founded the Black Panther Party to organise the black working class. They focused on two aspects of black liberation that had been highlighted by Malcolm X: self-defence and economic improvements (see Chapter 13). Black people needed an organised defence, the BPP argued, because they could not trust the police or the American justice system. According to Newton the police 'occupied' the black ghettos in the same way that the US army occupied areas of Vietnam. As a result, the Black Panther Party organised its own **militia** who patrolled black neighbourhoods, wearing a uniform including a black beret, blue shirt and black leather jackets. The rejection of the police was summed up in the Party slogan: 'Off the pigs!'

The BPP's second goal was to improve the conditions in northern ghettos. As a result, the Party organised campaigns to demand government investment in black neighbourhoods. The Party also organised welfare schemes to help improve the lives of African Americans in northern cities.

The Ten-Point Programme

The aims of the BPP were summarised in the Ten-Point Programme (see Source 15.1). The programme addressed a huge range of issues that Newton believed were necessary for the liberation of black people. Points 2, 5, 6 and

> ### Source 15.1: The Black Panthers Ten-Point Programme, published 15 October 1966.
>
> 1. We want power to determine the destiny of our black and oppressed communities' education that teaches us our true history and our role in the present day society.
> 2. We want completely free healthcare for all black and oppressed people.
> 3. We want an immediate end to police brutality and murder of black people, other people of color, all oppressed people inside the United States.
> 4. We want an immediate end to all wars of aggression.
> 5. We want full employment for our people.
> 6. We want an end to the robbery by the capitalists of our black community.
> 7. We want decent housing, fit for the shelter of human beings.
> 8. We want decent education for our people that exposes the true nature of this decadent American society.
> 9. We want freedom for all black and oppressed people now held in US Federal, state, county, city and military prisons and jails. We want trials by a jury of peers for all persons charged with so-called crimes under the laws of this country.
> 10. We want land, bread, housing, education, clothing, justice, peace and people's community control of modern technology.
>
> Taken from: *The Black Panthers Speak,* ed. Philip Sheldon Foner and Clayborne Carson (2002)

7 addressed the economic needs of black Americans, demanding decent healthcare, housing, employment and an end to economic exploitation. Points 3 and 9 concerned the safety and defence of black people. The demand for the immediate release of all black people may be difficult to understand, but it reflected the widely held belief that black people could not get a fair trial in America. Indeed, the Black Panthers' newspaper *Black Panther* contained numerous stories of police violence and miscarriages of justice to illustrate the racist nature of the US justice system.

Ideology

The Black Panthers, like Malcolm X, were black nationalists; that is to say they believed that black people should govern themselves. Newton and Seale combined this nationalism with an emphasis on anti-colonialism. Inspired by Frantz Fanon's *The Wretched of the Earth* (1961), they linked the black struggle for freedom in America with the fight against colonial domination in the Third World (countries in Africa, Latin America and Asia). As a result they looked to figures such as **Mao Zedong,** who had successfully expelled foreign white oppressors from China and established a revolutionary Chinese government. Newton and Seale stressed solidarity with oppressed people around the world and as a result opposed the Vietnam War, calling for black people to refuse to fight. Fanon's book also suggested that violence was essential in the struggle against colonial oppression. Newton and Seale agreed, arguing that the violent colonial oppression of the American state could only be successfully challenged by violent revolutionary action by black people.

Newton and Seale's emphasis on revolution came from a study of Marxism. The German philosopher **Karl Marx** argued that there could be no real freedom under **capitalism**. Freedom, he argued, could only be gained through revolution led by the working class. Newton and Seale followed this Marxist emphasis on the working class and attempted to organise the American black working class through the Black Panther Party.

Methods

'Patrol the pigs'

One of the Panthers' first initiatives was the 'patrol the pigs' campaign, which began in Oakland, California. Essentially the campaign was designed to keep the police under surveillance and in so doing protect African Americans from the abuse of police power. Any time a police patrol stopped or arrested an African American, Black Panther patrols would observe the incident. Newton himself was heavily involved in the campaign. He carried law books in his car and would intervene in any incident, questioning the police and drawing a crowd of onlookers. The campaign highlighted police abuses and educated local black residents regarding their legal rights. The campaign gained great support among the black population of Oakland and as a result the BPP grew and was able to expand the campaign to the Californian cities of Richmond and Berkeley.

Mao Zedong

(1893–1976)

Chinese revolutionary who adapted Marx's ideas to the Chinese situation and established a revolutionary government in 1949. He ruled China until his death in 1976.

Karl Marx

(1818–1883)

German philosopher and journalist who argued that the inequalities of capitalist society could be solved by a working-class revolution.

Take note

As you read through this section, in the second column of your table, make a note of the different aspects of the Black Panthers' ideology. Link these to the Panthers' demands from the Ten-Point Programme in the first column by placing them in the row next to the most appropriate objective.

Glossary:
Capitalism

An economic system where people aim to make a profit and goods and services are distributed according to wealth rather than need.

As you read through this section, add a third column to your table. Use this column to make a note of the Black Panthers' campaigns. Link the campaigns to the Panthers' objectives, for example the Free Huey campaign could be placed next to the Panthers' demand that all-black prisoners be released.

The Californian state government felt threatened by this campaign and attempted to ban Black Panther patrols. In response, the Panthers courted media attention, seeking to win further support for their cause. In this respect they were hugely successful, and by the end of 1967 the Party had become a national organisation with 35 different local groups across 15 states. The Panthers gained further publicity due to the 'Free Huey' campaign following Newton's arrest on murder charges in 1967. Newton was released in 1970 and the case was dropped.

Survival programmes

Newton's arrest led to new leadership and therefore a change in direction for the Black Panthers. From 1968 the Party emphasised welfare programmes rather than confrontations with the police. The late 1960s saw the launch of a series of 'survival programmes' that aimed to improve the lives of African Americans living in northern city ghettos. These programmes, which were planned in 1968, included:

- Free Breakfast for School Children Programme
- free health clinics
- free 'liberation schools'.

The programmes were funded by local black business people, as well as celebrities such as **Richard Pryor**, **Jimi Hendrix** and **James Brown**. The free breakfast campaign was highly successful, and by 1969 had expanded from its base at St Augustine's Church in Oakland to feed over 10,000 children each school day.

The health clinics were also a success. They offered tests for conditions predominantly affecting black people, such as the blood condition **sickle cell disease**. In addition, they offered emergency medical care and contraception advice. The free clinic idea became very popular and women's groups and groups supporting Hispanic Americans soon followed the Black Panthers' example. By 1974 there were 200 free clinics across the USA which treated over 200,000 people a year.

Black Panthers march in New York, July 1968, during the trial of Huey Newton in Oakland, California.

Richard Pryor

(1940–2005)

Multi-award winning comedian, actor and writer. Challenging racism was a constant theme in his work.

Jimi Hendrix

(1942–1970)

Innovative rock guitarist and singer. He is best remembered for his iconic performance at the Woodstock Festival of 1969.

The Oakland Community School was the first of the Black Panthers' liberation schools. Liberation schools were staffed by volunteers and

Led by their teacher, students in a Black Panther liberation school give the 'Black Power' salute, San Francisco, 1969.

located in church halls, the backs of shops or sometimes in people's homes. Initially, they aimed to empower adult black Americans by teaching them about the struggles, actions or the past achievements of black people. The focus on black history and culture was at odds with mainstream education and was designed to inspire self-confidence and a greater sense of identity in the students. However, as the number of schools increased, they began to admit children and young adults, and aimed to provide academic support to students in conventional education.

The Black Panthers were genuinely popular among America's young black working class. By 1968 the BPP had branches in Pittsburgh, Seattle, Los Angeles, Chicago, San Diego, Newark, Denver, New York City, Boston, Philadelphia, Washington D.C. and Baltimore. While the Black Panthers only had 5000 official members in 1968, their newspaper had a circulation of 250,000 and an estimated readership of a million. Moreover, by the end of the 1960s **Eldridge Cleaver**, Newton and Seale had a 70 per cent approval rating among black GIs serving in Vietnam.

Official persecution and the decline of the Black Panthers

Government authorities were extremely suspicious of the Black Panthers and therefore took a series of steps to try and combat the movement. The FBI led the way in attacking the Panthers. According to a memorandum produced by the FBI's counter-intelligence unit, COINTELPRO, the FBI believed a radical black leader or 'black messiah' would soon emerge who would unite radical groups, such as the Black Panthers, and lead black people in a violent revolution against the American government. The FBI's paranoia provided them with the justification they needed to mount a 'dirty tricks' campaign against the Party. For example, the FBI used techniques such as telephone tapping, bugging the offices and homes of leading members of the Party, arrests and infiltration in an attempt to weaken and destroy the movement. Additionally, the FBI forged letters in order to claim that the Black Panthers were sending death threats to senior government officials.

The FBI campaign was extremely damaging and led to a loss of support for the Party. Additionally, frequent arrests of leading members meant that the Black Panthers were spending an increasing amount of their money on legal fees to the detriment of the 'survival programmes.'

Disagreements among the leaders of the Black Panthers also led to a reduction in the influence of the Party. For example, there was tension between Newton and the Party's Presidential candidate Eldridge Cleaver on the use of violence. In 1968 Newton argued that the Party should play down the use of force and emphasise 'survival programmes'. Cleaver, on the other hand, remained committed to militancy. Additionally, female members of the Panthers objected to the macho image of the Party. There was conflict between the original male members who had joined a defence force and the new female recruits who were essential for running the health and education 'survival programmes.' Indeed, many women in the Party objected to the high profile given to Eldridge Cleaver who, prior to joining the Party, was a

James Brown

(1933–2006)

Pioneering soul singer, best known for songs such as *Sex machine*. His work remains highly influential.

Glossary:
Sickle cell disease

Also known as sickle cell anaemia, this is a lifelong blood disorder which means that blood has difficulty flowing around some parts of the body. The disease leads to organ damage and significantly shortens life expectancy.

Take note

As you work through this section, make notes on the reasons why the Black Panthers declined towards the end of the 1960s. You should make notes in two categories: (a) internal tensions; (b) external pressure.

Eldridge Cleaver

(1935–1998)

Eldridge Cleaver was a prominent member of the Black Panther Party. He rose to fame following the publication of his book *Soul on Ice* (1968). Following Newton's arrest, Cleaver became the leading member of the Black Panthers. He stood as the Peace and Freedom Party's candidate in the Presidential Election of 1968, polling 0.15 per cent of the popular vote.

convicted rapist. These internal divisions, along with politically motivated police persecution, sapped the Party's strength, and in 1977 the BPP disbanded.

Conclusion

The Black Panthers followed the path mapped out by Malcolm X. They shared his desire to stand up to racist authorities, and adopted his techniques, using the resources available within black communities to improve the lives of residents within these communities. Panther actions such as the 'patrol the pigs' campaign and the survival programmes were highly effective. However, the Party never succeeded in stamping out police racism. Rather, they themselves were to fall victim to the paranoid attacks of the FBI.

Activity: Ministry of Information

Taking it further

There are various short films about the Black Panthers on the Internet. Post a comment on one, assessing its usefulness for historians studying the impact of the movement.

You could go even further, using footage from the Internet to make your own documentary on the Panthers. You could do this using Microsoft Movie Maker, which will allow you to edit video, put your own sound track to the footage and add a voiceover in which you explain what the Panthers did and why it was significant.

Divide into small groups. You are activists working in the Black Panthers' press office. Each group should create a poster and a press release to publicise one of the following issues of the BPP's campaigns:

- the survival programmes
- protests about the shooting of Bobby Hutton
- the 'Free Huey' campaign
- the recruitment campaign to attract more members
- Eldridge Cleaver's Presidential Election Campaign.

Having created these materials, present them to the rest of the class. The whole class should assess the materials in terms of the following criteria:

	Mark out of 10
How eye-catching the posters are	
How detailed the press releases are	
How accurately they reflect the Black Panthers' ideas	
How effectively they promote the Black Panthers' campaigns	

Chapter 16 **The achievement of the Black Power movement**

Key questions

- What problems faced black Americans in urban areas in the late 1960s?
- What were the social and economic achievements of the Black Power movement?
- What impact did Black Power have on black identity and American culture?

America was proud of its status as a democracy. By the time the Black Panthers were founded in 1966, all adult citizens – regardless of race or gender – could vote in elections to choose state and federal leaders. However, to activists in the Black Power movement, this was not enough. They had a much richer idea of what democracy meant. To them, America could not be a democracy until black Americans had power over black communities. This radical view of democracy was to become highly influential across the protest movements of the late 1960s and is a lasting legacy of Black Power.

Timeline

1965	Los Angeles riot SNCC establishes the 'Freedom City' in Mississippi Black actor Bill Cosby cast in a leading TV role
1966	SNCC starts The Free D.C. Movement *Star Trek* is first screened, starring black actor Nichelle Nichols
1967	Newark, Detroit and New Brunswick riots The Mississippi 'Freedom City' project ends Black actor Eartha Kitt cast as Catwoman in TV series *Batman*
1968	Black athletes give Black Power salute at the Olympic Games
1971	The film *Sweet Sweetback's Baadassssss Song* is released Gordon Parks' film *Shaft* is released
1972	National Sickle Cell Anemia Control Act passed by Congress

Political and economic achievements of Black Power

Black Power did not solve the social and economic problems facing northern blacks. Indeed, it was unrealistic to expect it to provide a solution to such huge issues in such a short period. But it did offer practical help to black people living in the ghettos as well as ensuring that the problems remained on the political agenda.

Organising northern blacks

Martin Luther King's Southern Christian Leadership Conference (SCLC) proved to be highly effective in mobilising southern blacks. However, King's Christian message did not have the same appeal to blacks living in northern

Take note

Using your own knowledge gained from previous chapters, in the centre of a piece of paper make a list of the social and economic problems facing black Americans in the 1960s. Around the outside of the page, make a list of the achievements of the Black Power movement. Draw lines between them to show how the Black Power movement tried to resolve the social and economic problems facing black citizens.

Marion Barry

(born 1936)

Activist and politician, Barry was the first chairman of the Student Nonviolent Coordinating Committee (SNCC). During the 1960s he completed a PhD in chemistry, but left academia due to the fact that white parents refused to let him teach their children. He was mayor of Washington D.C. from 1979 to 1991 and again from 1995–1999.

Take note

As you read through this section, on the left-hand side of a page, list the characteristics of the new black identity championed by the Black Power movement. This can be done as a bullet list.

ghettos who had deserted the Church. Equally, King's approach appealed much more to the middle class than it did to working-class black people. The Student Nonviolent Coordinating Committee (SNCC) and the Black Panthers, with their stress on self-defence and their commitment to addressing the economic problems of the ghettos, were much more attractive to northern working-class blacks. Consequently, both groups were able to organise high-profile campaigns in order to address the issues facing northern black communities.

Freedom Cities – organising black people for Black Power

Malcolm X, Stokely Carmichael and the Black Panthers shared a vision of black people controlling their own communities. SNCC's Free D.C. Movement, headed by **Marion Barry**, was one highly successful example. It aimed to bring 'home rule' to the black community of Washington D.C. The project started in 1966 with demonstrations against the way the local schools were administered. By the end of 1966 the black citizens of Washington D.C. had won the right to elect their own school boards. Barry was also involved in setting up a 'Model Police Precinct' controlled by a police board partly elected by the local black community. SNCC's work gained $3 million worth of government funding to improve community policing.

SNCC pioneered similar radical projects across America. In New York, a SNCC campaign saw black people take control of the Intermediate School 201 in Harlem. The 'Freedom City' in Mississippi also enjoyed some success. SNCC, working with local churches, set up the Child Development Group of Mississippi. The group raised $1.5 million from the churches and the federal government to set up 85 Head Start centres to support young children. The project faced enormous opposition from Ross R. Barnett, the racist state governor, and from Senator John C. Stennis, a long-standing opponent of integration. On hearing that SNCC radicals were involved in the project, Stennis demanded an end to government aid. In spite of these attacks, the project lasted from 1965 to 1967 and improved the lives of thousands of black people in Mississippi.

Black Panther initiatives

The Black Panthers' educational and health initiatives helped tens of thousands of people in the late 1960s. One of their best-known campaigns concerned sickle cell anaemia, a medical condition that predominantly affects black people. By the end of the decade there were 49 Black Panther clinics across America. The Illinois People's Free Medical Care Centre set up by the BPP, for example, treated 2000 people in its first two months alone. Prior to the Panthers' campaign, little was known about the condition and the US government had no strategy for dealing with the disease. However, the Panther's campaign brought the illness to the nation's attention and in 1972 the government passed the National Sickle Cell Anemia Control Act, committing government money to the research and treatment of the disease.

Black identity

Black Power's most profound triumph was remaking black identity. Slavery and segregation had taken a terrible toll on African Americans. Slavery uprooted Africans from their homeland and also separated them from their history. Enslavement stripped black people of their independence and their pride, and robbed them of their identity. Malcolm X summed up the problem memorably when he remarked 'the worst crime the white man has committed has been to teach us to hate ourselves.'

Radicals, particularly in SNCC and the Black Panthers, recognised the need for black people to understand themselves differently – to forge a new independent identity. Consequently, Stokely Carmichael and Huey P. Newton emphasised the study of black history in order to connect African Americans with their past and provide them with examples of powerful black figures. SNCC, the Black Panthers and Malcolm X also stressed the need for black Americans to recognise their African heritage. Moreover, African history was full of examples of radical black groups overthrowing oppressors and gaining independence for themselves. Recovering the past and recognising that they were part of a global struggle with Africa at its heart was crucial to the development of self-esteem, self-respect, independence and pride for many young African Americans.

New identities took many forms. Malcolm X, for example, adopted the surname X in recognition that his original African name was lost, while Stokely Carmichael took on the African name Kwame Ture out of respect for the Ghanaian revolutionary leader and first head of state of independent Ghana, Kwame Nkrumah. The Afro hairstyle also became a popular symbol of black identity. The style was associated with black radical **Angela Davis**.

This change in identity fundamentally altered the American vocabulary. For generations black people had been known as 'Negroes' or as 'colored' – terms that were associated with slavery and segregation. Activists in the Black Power movement rejected these terms and referred to themselves as 'black.' This positive control of language was highly influential and by the end of the 1960s the terms 'Negro' and 'colored' had fallen into disuse.

Angela Davis

(born 1944)

A member of SNCC and a campaigner for black rights, women's rights and gay rights. She became Professor of Philosophy at the University of California, Los Angeles, in 1969. In 1970 she became involved with a Black Panther plot to free a number of high-profile black prisoners. As a result she became the third woman in American history to feature on the FBI's top ten most wanted list. She was captured after a two-month FBI hunt but acquitted of all charges at the end of her trial in 1972.

Political activist and philosophy professor, Angela Davis, wearing an Afro hairstyle.

Miles Davis

(1926–1991)

One of the most influential musicians and composers of the twentieth century. His career began in the 1940s and continued into the early 1990s. He pioneered a number of new musical styles, notably in the 1960s he mixed jazz with electric instruments and then with electronica.

Bill Cosby

(born 1937)

Comedian, author, media producer and civil rights activist. He is probably best known for *The Cosby Show*, a sit-com that ran from 1984–1992. During this period Cosby was the highest paid entertainer on American television. Cosby also helped to finance the 1971 film *Sweet Sweetback's Baadasssss Song*, which depicts the Black Panthers' fight against police brutality in downtown Los Angeles.

The cultural impact of the Black Power movement

Black music

Black Power had a profound effect on black music. The jazz composer and musician **Miles Davis** is an excellent example of the cultural changes caused by Black Power. At around the same time that SNCC and the Congress of Racial Equality (CORE) excluded white members, Davis formed an all-black band. Similarly, at the same time that SNCC and the Black Panthers were emphasising black history and African culture, Davis's albums began to use more non-Western instruments and incorporate ideas from traditional African music as well as modern black styles pioneered by black artists such as James Brown and Jimi Hendrix. Davis also fought with his record company to have pictures of black women on his album covers. Traditionally, record companies had chosen images of white women, but albums such as *E.S.P.* (1965) changed this. *Bitches Brew* at the end of the 1960s went further, the cover being based on imagery from traditional African art.

Media portrayal of black Americans

Black Power also changed the way in which black people were portrayed in the media. NBC Television's *Star Trek*, for example, broke new ground by including a highly trained and technically competent black character, Lieutenant Uhura, played by Nichelle Nichols. The fictional character clearly reflected the new emphasis on African identity as she came from Africa, spoke Swahili and had a name derived from the Swahili word *uhuru*, meaning 'freedom'. *Star Trek* featured an inter-racial kiss between Uhura and Captain Kirk. The kiss caused a political storm and was only the second inter-racial kiss in American television history.

Eartha Kitt's Catwoman – a character in the ABC television series *Batman* – was an even more striking example of a powerful, assertive black character. Kitt, who had risen to fame as a singer and actor in the 1950s, was a well-known advocate of black rights. A final example is **Bill Cosby**'s role in the series *I Spy,* which ran on American television from 1965–1968. Cosby, a black actor, comedian, writer and civil rights activist, played a highly educated Pentagon spy.

In film, too, there was a radical shift in the portrayal of black characters. Melvin Van Peebles' *Sweet Sweetback's Baadasssss Song* (1971) dramatised the story of a Black Panther and graphically depicted the racist violence of the Los Angeles police. Huey Newton praised the film and organised screenings for new members of the Black Panthers. The film was a box office hit and as a result more mainstream movies were made reflecting the new powerful black identity. *Shaft* (1971) is the best-known example. The film tells the story of a black private detective who teams up with the Black Panthers to defeat the New York mafia and save the city from a race riot. The film was a mainstream success.

Black athletes Tommie Smith and John Carlos kept Black Power in the news. The men gave a 'power to the people' salute during the 1968 Mexico City

Olympics while receiving their medals for the 200 metres race. The athletes used the event to make a series of symbolic points. Gold medalist Smith wore a black scarf around his neck representing black pride. Carlos, who won the bronze medal, wore a necklace of beads symbolising the black Americans who had been lynched and killed in race crimes. Both athletes wore no shoes as a symbol of the solidarity with those in poverty in Africa. The Olympic Committee were outraged at the gesture and demanded that the American team suspend both athletes.

Conclusion

The Black Power movement had an enormous impact on American culture and society. Activists such as Malcolm X, Stokely Carmichael, Huey P. Newton and Bobby Seale helped to forge a radical new identity for black people and changed race relations forever. The emphasis on pride and self-help led to ground-breaking democratic experiments such as the Free D.C. Movement and the sickle cell campaign. However, the high-profile campaigns of SNCC and the Black Panthers also drew the attention of racist opponents such as Senator Stennis, who used their influence to stop community projects that involved activists. Nonetheless, the radicalism and courage of black activists became a model for protestors from all backgrounds. Hispanic Americans, Native Americans and women all adopted their methods to return power to the people.

> **Taking it further**
>
> The idea of black history was crucial for many of the Black Power organisations. Search the Internet to find a video clip showing Darcus Howe explaining what the term means. Then write a paragraph in answer to the question: 'What is the relationship between black history and revolutionary politics?'

Activity: Black Power web

Imagine that you have been asked to research and design a website recording the achievements of Black Power. You should design a site consisting of:

a) a home page

b) a black identity page

c) a black culture page

d) a black politics page

e) a life in the ghetto page.

Skills Builder 3: Writing introductions and conclusions

When answering questions in Unit 1, students will be expected to write an essay. So far, in Skills Builder 1, you have learned the importance of writing in paragraphs and, in Skills Builder 2, you have learned about the importance of showing a clear argument when answering questions on causation and change.

In this section, you will look at the importance of writing introductory and concluding paragraphs.

In your essay you will be answering a specific question. Your answer must be:
- directly relevant to the question
- supported by relevant historical information
- in the form of an argument that provides a historical analysis of the question.

When writing under examination conditions you should spend approximately 40 minutes on the whole of your essay. During this time you must:
- plan what you are going to write
- write a separate paragraph for each major point you wish to make
- check through what you have written.

Therefore, given the time constraints, you should not spend more than five minutes writing your introduction.

What should you put in your introduction?

Your introduction should answer the question directly and set out what you plan to cover and discuss in your essay. Your introduction needs to show that you will answer the question in an analytical way – and that you haven't just started writing without thinking. Therefore, it is good to say, very briefly, what you are going to argue in the essay. You can then refer back to your introduction as you write to make sure that your argument is on track.

We are going to look at an introduction to an answer to the following question:

(A) How far do you agree that differences in personality were the main cause of the divisions in the civil rights movement in the late 1960s?

This question gives one of the reasons for the divisions in the civil rights movement and it asks 'how far' you agree that it was the most important reason. This question will require you to assess other reasons why the divisions occurred and make a judgement about the significance of each of these reasons.

Here is an example of an introduction that you might write:

Differences in personality were certainly one of the reasons for the divisions in the civil rights movement in the late 1960s. However, it cannot be described as the main reason because this overlooks the significance of differences in aims between the different groups. Although many factors contributed to the divisions in the civil rights movement, for example disagreements over collaboration between races, attitudes to the law, and whether or not to use violence – it was disagreements over the aims of the movement which were the primary cause of divisions within the civil rights movement. The disagreement over aims was crucial because without a common goal, there was no reason for the groups to work together.

This introduction answers the question directly. It recognises that the divisions in the civil rights movement had a number of causes, it states these causes, and briefly explains which factor was most important and why.

Activity: Spot the mistake

The following introductions have been written in response to the question above. Each one illustrates a common mistake. Spot them!

Example 1:

There were many reasons why the civil rights movement became divided in the late 1960s. Personality clashes were one reason. Other reasons include differences over aims, such as integration or separatism, differences over methods, such as peaceful or violent protest, and the black response to the Vietnam War. In this essay, I will consider all of these factors and will reach a judgement about which was most important.

Example 2:

During the Montgomery bus boycott of 1955–1956, Martin Luther King emerged as the leader of the civil rights movement. King promoted a nonviolent form of protest, encouraging black Americans to use legal methods to fight for legal equality. These methods were very successful and resulted in the Civil Rights Act of 1964 and the Voting Rights Act of 1965. However, in the early 1960s, a group called the Nation of Islam started calling for more violent methods to be used and criticised the aim of integration. The spokesman for the Nation of Islam was Malcolm X, who described Martin Luther King as an 'Uncle Tom'.

Example 3:

Differences in personality were the major cause of the divisions in the civil rights movement in the late 1960s. Martin Luther King was a high-profile leader, but not everybody agreed with him. Stokely Carmichael, leader of SNCC, resented the way in which King wanted to dominate SNCC campaigns. Similarly, radicals within SNCC and CORE thought that King was too conservative. The NAACP refused to work with Carmichael and SNCC following Carmichael's verbal attack on the organisation in 1966. Finally, Malcolm X's influence led Huey P. Newton and Bobby Searle to found the Black Panther Party in 1966.

Answers:

Example 1 – this introduction includes a range of factors, but does not indicate a line of argument. The last sentence adds nothing to the answer and wastes examination time.

Example 2 – this introduction gives background information about the topic, but it does not answer the question.

Example 3 – this introduction considers personalities alone, and does not mention any other factors. Therefore, it is unbalanced and does not show a broad range of knowledge.

It is important that your essay does not contradict your introduction. If you state in your introduction that disagreements over aims was the most important factor, then you must maintain this argument throughout your essay, even when discussing the other factors involved.

Introduction: DOs and DON'Ts
- DO look at the question and decide on your line of argument.
- DO make reference to the question in your introduction.
- DO show what you intend to argue.
- DON'T begin your answer by writing a story.
- DON'T spend too long writing your introduction. Five minutes is enough.

Activity: Write your own introduction

Write an introduction to the following question:

> (B) How far do you agree that Black Power achieved little for black Americans?

Why are conclusions important?

When you are asked a question in the examination, you are expected to answer it! The concluding paragraph is very important in this process. It should summarise the argument you have made, with your verdict on the question. It should not be more than three or four sentences in length, and under examination conditions it should take no more than five minutes to write.

Here is an example conclusion for Question A:

Divisions in the civil rights movement in the late 1960s were the result of a range of factors, such as differences in aims, personality clashes, disagreement over collaboration between races, attitudes to the law, and whether or not to use violence. However, the main reason for the divisions was differences in aims rather than personality clashes. Clearly, there were tensions between leading personalities within the movement, but in the early 1960s, when there was general agreement on the need to end segregation, groups such as the NAACP, SNCC and SCLC were able to work together. In the late 1960s, following the radicalisation of SNCC, there was considerable disagreement over the aims of the movement and this lack of common ground divided the movement.

Activity: Write your own conclusion

Using Question B above write a conclusion of approximately four sentences. Try to write it in five minutes.

Activity: Write an introduction and a conclusion

Here is another example of a question:

> (C) How far do you agree that the major consequence of divisions within the civil rights movement was that progress towards racial equality slowed down?

Now write an introduction and conclusion to this question, each in approximately five minutes.

Chapter 17 **Mainstream and counterculture in the 1960s**

Key questions

- What were the key features of mainstream American culture in the 1960s?
- What was distinctive about youth culture in the 1960s?
- What were the different cultural and political aspects of the counterculture?

Scooby-Doo, America's best-loved cartoon dog, is a 'child of the Sixties'. Created in 1969 Scooby and the rest of his gang of teen detectives reflect an important split in sixties American culture. Fred looks like the captain of the football team and Daphne could easily be the high school prom queen. They represent mainstream American culture. Shaggy and Velma on the other hand represent the counterculture. Shaggy, for example, wears hippie flares and a beatnik v-neck, while Velma wears a short skirt, has short hair, not to mention being brainy, independent and, compared with Daphne at least, a bit of a feminist. The characters are stereotypes, but in spite of this they demonstrate the split between the mainstream and the counterculture, which stressed an alternative way of life based on love and peace.

Timeline

1957	Publication of *Mass Culture and the Popular Arts*
1960	John F. Kennedy elected President
1961	Peace Corps established
1962	Publication of *The Other America*
1963	Assassination of President Kennedy; Lyndon B. Johnson becomes President
1965	Social Security Act
1968	Apollo 8 circles the Moon
1969	Apollo 11 lands on the Moon

Glossary:

Inflation

A process that leads to the price of goods increasing over time.

Gross national product

A measure of the total wealth produced by a nation in one year.

White collar occupation

Non-manual, professional occupation.

Middle class

Typically used to describe workers in white collar occupations.

Introduction

The late 1950s and early 1960s was a time of unparalleled wealth for the majority of Americans. Nonetheless, the period also witnessed the growth of a counterculture that challenged some of America's deepest traditions.

'Populuxe'

From 1945 to 1960 the USA enjoyed continual economic growth. The 1950s was a period of low **inflation** and negligible unemployment. America's **gross national product** grew from $300,000 million in 1950 to $500,000 million a decade later.

By 1956, 60 per cent of Americans worked in **white collar occupations**. During the 1950s and 1960s, the number of Americans who owned their own homes increased significantly: by 1960, 61.9 per cent of homes were owner occupied, compared with 43.6 per cent in 1940.

Many working-class Americans also prospered during this period. Labour unions were able to use their power to negotiate excellent deals for their members and as a result the wages for production workers leapt by 70 per cent between 1950 and 1970. The new wealth created a consumer boom. The number of car owners rose dramatically: in 1940, one in five Americans owned a car; by 1970 the figure was one in two. By 1960 some commentators believed America had entered an age of populuxe – that is, a time when everyone could afford to live in some measure of luxury.

The politics of affluence

The **Great Depression** had reduced many Americans to poverty. As a result, Americans had been cautious during this period, holding on to the wealth that they had while fearing that depression could strike again. Many Americans had believed that in order for others to benefit, they would have to lose. In this atmosphere it is not surprising that many white Americans were suspicious of anything that would make the lives of black citizens better. However, the affluence of the period made the middle classes feel more secure and therefore less anxious about greater opportunities for black people.

Young people were also affected by the prolonged period of affluence. '**Baby boomers**' had never known poverty or economic depression. Additionally, the young people of the 1960s were better educated than any generation before them. Consequently, they were both less materialistic and more interested in political issues. Therefore, while they consumed more, they were more willing to contemplate making sacrifices for a good cause. Youthful idealism was sometimes expressed in the counterculture and the liberal politics and idealism of Kennedy's presidency.

Liberal politics

Kennedy's 'New Frontier'

At 43, John F. Kennedy was the youngest man ever to be elected President. Politically, Kennedy was an inspirational figure. He launched a number of ground-breaking initiatives that appealed to the ambition and optimism of young people, urging them to 'Ask not what your country can do for you – ask what you can do for your country.'

First, in 1961 Kennedy established the Peace Corps, an organisation which sent volunteers to work in the developing world. He also committed the government to a multi-billion dollar space programme with the aim of landing a man on the Moon by the end of the 1960s. Both of these projects appealed to the ideals of self-sacrifice and ambition, as well as showing that the new President was looking towards the challenges of the future. Both programmes were highly successful. By 1966 over 15,000 volunteers were working overseas as part of the Peace Corps and in 1969 the Apollo Programme successfully landed two men on the Moon.

Glossary:

Great Depression

A period of worldwide economic crisis from 1929–1945, marked by high unemployment and widespread poverty.

'Baby boomers'

A generation born in the period following the Second World War. 'Baby boomers' are associated with a period of relative wealth and privilege, growing up healthy, wealthy and optimistic about the future.

Take note

Draw the table below. In the first column make a note of the aims of the two Presidents of the period – Kennedy and Johnson. Then note their successes and failures in the next two columns. Finally, write a summary paragraph for each President summarising the extent to which they achieved their aims.

President's aims	Successes	Failures

However, Kennedy's domestic policies were not as spectacular. He described his vision for America as the 'New Frontier' and aimed to introduce better healthcare and increase funding for education. However, Kennedy was forced to work with a Congress that was dominated by Republicans and conservative southern Democrats. Congress blocked many of Kennedy's policies, such as his Medical Health Bill.

Johnson's 'Great Society'

Lyndon B. Johnson was much less glamorous than Kennedy, but he too had a vision of a more equal society. He wanted the USA to be a 'Great Society' as well as a rich one. He believed the government should use some of America's new-found wealth to improve the lives of America's poor. From 1964 to 1966 Johnson worked with Congress to pass 435 bills which committed $1.5 billion to improve schools and $2.9 billion to regenerate America's inner cities. In addition, his 1965 Social Security Act guaranteed free healthcare to all people aged 65 and over.

The failure of liberalism

Kennedy and Johnson both spoke of a fairer society. However, neither President was able to deliver the reform that idealistic young Americans wanted. Kennedy was slow to act on civil rights. Johnson had more success, but the **Vietnam War** distracted his attention and diverted government money from his 'Great Society' programme. Additionally, the Vietnam War alienated many young idealists who had initially supported Kennedy and Johnson.

Mass culture

Media culture

The 1950s and 1960s witnessed the emergence of a mass American culture in which music, books, newspapers, films and television programmes were mass produced and consumed by much of American society. The number of televisions in American homes jumped from 10.3 million in 1951 to 34.9 million in 1956. By 1960, 90 per cent of Americans owned a television and watched news, programmes and adverts.

America's original diverse culture became dominated by a new media culture. This phenomenon was analysed in Bernard Rosenberg and David Manning White's book *Mass Culture: The Popular Arts in America* (1957). Rosenberg and White argued that modern mass culture deliberately filled the minds of Americans with worthless ideas and in so doing distracted them from real issues, such as poverty.

Corporate culture

Another aspect of American mass culture was the corporate culture of the 1950s and 1960s. Following the Second World War, the American economy became dominated by large companies. In 1940, the USA's biggest hundred companies were responsible for 30 per cent of the country's manufacture; by the end of the Second World War this figure had increased to 70 per cent. The dominance of these large companies significantly changed American culture. Traditionally, American culture stressed independence and individualism.

Glossary:

Vietnam War

A conflict between Communist forces in North Vietnam and anti-Communist forces in South Vietnam. The American government sent large-scale military support to South Vietnam between 1965 and 1973.

Take note

Based on what you have read so far in this chapter, write a detailed paragraph in answer to the question: 'How widespread was prosperity in America in the 1960s?'

Take note

Summarise:
1. the two essential beliefs that were common across America's counterculture in the 1960s.
2. the values of America's counterculture.

Glossary:

Hippy

A person who is part of a youth subculture that emerged in the 1960s. The first hippies rejected mainstream culture and established alternative communities in which they practised 'free love' (sex outside of marriage) and experimented with drugs.

Peacenik

A term of abuse used to describe an anti-war campaigner.

However, big businesses valued loyalty and conformity. This conformity was deeply unattractive to American youth and one of the reasons why they turned to protest.

The other America

Not everyone gained during this boom period. Michael Harrington's *The Other America* (1962) presented an analysis of American society which showed the limits of 'populuxe' society. Harrington demonstrated that poverty was still present in America and that certain groups, such as black people and the elderly, were largely excluded from the consumer boom. American society had become richer, but it had not become more equal. Indeed, in 1970 the poorest fifth of America's population received only 5 per cent of national wealth, whereas the richest fifth enjoyed 40 per cent of the country's wealth.

Counterculture

Timeline

1955	The Hollywood film *Rebel Without a Cause* is released
1959	William S. Burroughs publishes the novel *Naked Lunch*
1960	Students for a Democratic Society (SDS) formed at the University of Michigan
1962	SDS release the Port Huron Statement
1964	The Free Speech Movement is founded at the University of California
	President Johnson sends American troops to Vietnam
1965	SDS organise the first mass rally against the Vietnam War
1966	The anarchist Diggers establish a hippie commune in San Francisco
1967	The Beatles release *Sergeant Pepper's Lonely Hearts Club Band*
1968	Democrat National Convention Anti-War Riots
	Richard Nixon is elected President of the USA
1969	The Woodstock Festival
	Disney's film *Fantasia* re-released
1971	Kent State, Ohio, shootings followed by mass student demonstrations across USA
1975	End of the Vietnam War

Counterculture ideology

America's counterculture was not a coherent movement. It was made up of **hippies** and Black Panthers, feminists and **peaceniks**. As a result there was no single set of ideas that all of these different groups shared. Nonetheless, in general, countercultural groups agreed on two things. First they believed that America was corrupt. They thought that the ideals that politicians claimed to believe in, like peace, justice and freedom, were just empty words. They believed that, in reality, America was an unfree and unjust society and that the people with power wanted to keep it that way. Second, they believed that traditional political institutions such as political parties and elections could not deliver radical change. Consequently, they followed the lead of black activists and took their protest to the streets.

Disney

The Walt Disney Company was founded in 1923 by Walt Disney. It initially produced cartoons featuring characters such as Mickey Mouse and Donald Duck. The company made films and television programmes. It has become one of the most successful media and entertainment companies in the world.

Disney and the origins of America's counterculture

The American counterculture of the 1960s had its origins in the youth culture of the 1940s and 1950s. At the end of the Second World War a new social group emerged: teenagers. Teenagers were targeted by television stations and film companies. **Disney** films and television programmes, part of the new mass culture, were particularly popular during this period.

Disney films contained many countercultural values. First, Disney films popularised rock music. *The Mickey Mouse Club*, a television show that ran from 1955 to 1959 on America's ABC network, featured rock 'n' roll music every week. Second, Disney cartoons often contained dance scenes derived from Latin or African dance. For example, *The Three Caballeros*, a Disney film from 1944, contains an extended scene in which Donald Duck learns to 'loosen up' and take part in a Hispanic street party. Third, Disney films often contained psychedelic sequences that influenced the 'trippy' art and culture that came out of the Sixties drug culture. Counterculture hero, **Dr Timothy Leary**, who popularised the use of hallucinogenic drugs, claims that he was inspired to experiment with drugs after watching Disney's psychedelic *Fantasia* (1940), particularly the celebrated 'Magic Mushroom' sequence. *Fantasia* was re-released in 1969 and marketed as 'the ultimate trip'. Finally, Disney's heroes are often young rebels who stand up to mainstream culture. Disney's *The Story of Robin Hood and His Merrie Men* (1952) is a classic example of this. Robin Hood steals from the rich to give to the poor and stands up to the corrupt government in the form of the Sheriff of Nottingham. Walt Disney himself commented that Robin Hood 'remains an inspiration to all who love freedom'. The rock music, the carnival dancing, the trippy psychedelia and the young rebels who stood up to authority were all features of America's counterculture.

Youth culture: Sex, drugs and rock 'n' roll

By the end of the 1950s it was estimated that American teenagers spent $10 billion a year. Consequently, businesses rushed to get a piece of the teenage market by producing clothes, magazines, films, television programmes, cosmetics and music deliberately designed to appeal to young people. During the late 1950s and the 1960s there was increasing polarisation between the experimental culture of young people and the conservative mainstream culture of the older generation.

Don't stop the rock!

The influence of rock 'n' roll

Rock music was the big news of Sixties youth culture. The rock 'n' roll craze

Take note

Draw the following table. As you read through this section, list the different aspects of America's counterculture in the left-hand column of the table. In the right-hand column, make detailed notes on how these values were evident in Disney's films from the 1940s and 1950s.

The values of America's counterculture	Examples from Disney films

Dr Timothy Leary

(1920–1996)

Professor of Psychology at Harvard University and advocate of drug use. He was sacked from Harvard University after being found using drugs. He set up two communities dedicated to investigating the effects of LSD.

Source 17.1: Timothy Leary speaking at a protest against the banning of LSD in 1967.

Tune in, turn on, drop out.

Take note

Make a bullet-pointed list of the information in this section concerning American youth culture. Then write a sentence explaining why a youth culture emerged in the USA in the 1950s and 1960s.

Take note

As you read the sections on music and outsiders, make notes on:

1. the different aspects of youth culture in the 1960s
2. why older people were concerned about youth culture.

William S. Burroughs

(1914–1997)

Artist and novelist who used experimental techniques to write his novels. He wrote *Naked Lunch* in the so-called Beat Hotel in Paris which was the centre of a community of artists who experimented with drugs and free love. He used the $3,000 advance on *Naked Lunch* to buy drugs.

got going with **Elvis Presley**, the best known pop idol of the 1950s and 1960s. Presley's style mixed black gospel and blues music with white-Southern country music. His performances shocked conservative opinion who described his dance style as 'sexhibitionist'. White Citizens' Councils were horrified by rock music. Boston Church leader Rev. John Carroll claimed that 'rock 'n' roll inflames and excites youth like jungle tom-toms readying warriors for battle.' Nonetheless, record companies kept producing rock 'n' roll because teenagers kept buying it. By 1958, 70 per cent of all records sold were bought by teenagers. The British band **The Beatles** dominated the music scene in 1960s America. The Beatles were viewed by conservative Americans as even more worrying than Elvis, because of their rebelliousness and due to the fact that their 1967 album *Sergeant Pepper's Lonely Hearts Club Band* was clearly influenced by hallucinogenic drugs.

Elvis Presley

(1935–1977)

Dubbed the 'King of Rock 'n' Roll', Presley was an actor, singer and musician. He is one of the bestselling and most influential artists in the history of music. He pioneered rock music in the 1950s with records such as 'Hound Dog' and 'Jailhouse Rock'. During the 1960s he made 31 hit movies. He died in 1977.

The Beatles

Known as the 'Fab Four', the Beatles were a rock group from Liverpool made up of John Lennon, Paul McCartney, George Harrison and Ringo Starr. They formed in 1960 and split up in 1970. During the late 1960s they experimented with psychedelic music. In 2004 *Rolling Stone* magazine rated the Beatles as the best group of all time.

Outsiders

Glamorous outsiders were an important part of youth culture in the 1960s. Films and novels that appealed to young people often focused on a mismatch between the young heroes and the society they found themselves in. Stars like James Dean and Marlon Brando specialised in playing attractive outsiders. In the 1955 film *Rebel Without a Cause*, James Dean played a teenager who rejects the authority of his parents and his school teachers.

Beatniks

The **beatniks** grew out of the so-called 'beat generation' – a group of writers who questioned traditional American morality and encouraged their readers to experiment with drugs and sex in new ways. **William S. Burroughs**' *Naked Lunch* (1959), for example, described the journey of a drug addict across America. Beatniks rejected the 'populuxe' lifestyle of material plenty and focused on non-material things such as hallucinogenic experiences, sex, philosophy and poetry. They also rejected the '**square**' American work ethic in favour of leisure in which to read, think and experiment with art and life. The beatnik philosophy was reflected in the way they dressed. The media stereotype of the beatniks in the early 1960s was of men with goatees, sunglasses, black tops, berets and shoulder length hair who used phrases such as 'like cool man.' Female beatniks often had short hair, wore short skirts or trousers. The fashion for male beatniks to have long hair and female beatniks to have short hair indicated their rejection of traditional gender roles. The number of beatniks was never very large, but their ideas and their style influenced the hippies.

Hippies: Let's get together

By the mid 1960s, hippies (also known as 'flower-children', 'freaks' or 'longhairs') were the most prominent feature of America's counterculture. Hippie communities provided a refuge for young people who had run away from home. They also rejected traditional ideas of ownership in favour of co-operatives or communes in which goods were shared. The Diggers in San Francisco, for example, set up a money-free community in which goods and services were traded or given away for free. The Diggers' **anarchist** commune lasted from 1966 to 1968. By 1967 they had a free food store in Golden Gate Park, a free transport network, free healthcare and even put on free rock concerts featuring bands such as the Grateful Dead. Drugs and 'liberated' sexual relationships were also part of the communal experience. The Diggers so-called underground chemist, Owsley Stanley, produced large quantities of free LSD for hippies in the city.

Hippies rejected the artificial mass-produced mainstream culture in favour of a more natural culture. This was reflected in the hippy look which used natural fabrics, handmade clothes and long hair. The hippies, like the beatniks, were predominantly from middle-class backgrounds. Indeed, according to the organisers of Woodstock, the biggest hippie festival of the 1960s, not a single cheque for festival tickets bounced. Clearly, the hippies who went to Woodstock were not short of cash.

Student rebels: The New Left

The hippies and beatniks were cultural movements. The **New Left**, on the other hand, was more political. Mainstream American politicians were highly critical of socialism and communism: ideas associated with the Soviet Union, America's Cold War enemy. However, during the 1960s many students began to question this traditional attitude. What is more, radicals were also critical of the huge inequalities in wealth that existed in American society. Communism and socialism stressed economic equality and therefore became highly attractive to young radicals.

The first prominent New Left group was Students for a Democratic Society (SDS), a student group that formed at the University of Michigan in 1960. Many SDS members had been part of radical civil rights groups such as SNCC. SDS set out their aims in the Port Huron Statement of 1962. The Statement committed SDS to fight for a genuinely democratic society, in which each 'individual shares in those decisions which determine the quality and direction of his life'. It also advocated economic equality. Indeed, SDS argued that the economy should aim to provide a good life for all people rather than making profit.

Glossary:
Beatnik

The beatniks were a countercultural movement among young people in the late 1950s and early 1960s. The word 'beatnik' was first used in the *San Francisco Chronicle* in 1958. The word 'nik' is a reference to the Soviet satellite Sputnik – the first ever artificial spacecraft, and indicates that the beat culture was considered un-American.

Square

A word used by beatniks to describe mainstream American culture. It implies that mainstream culture is dull and unadventurous.

Anarchist

A political radical who wants government to be abolished.

Glossary:
New Left

The term used by radicals, often young people and university students, who campaigned for a more equal distribution of wealth in the USA. They used the term to distinguish themselves from the Communist Party of America, who they described as the 'Old Left.'

Mario Savio

(1942–1994)

Leader of the FSM and a former member of SNCC who was involved in the Mississippi Freedom Summer campaign of 1964. He campaigned for educational reform until his death in 1994.

A second New Left student group was based at the University of California, Berkeley. Students at the University of California had a reputation for being involved in radical politics: approximately 10 per cent of the students had taken part in civil rights protests between 1960 and 1964. On 1 October 1964, the University authorities declared that handing out political leaflets on campus was forbidden. As a result the students established the Free Speech Movement (FSM) to fight the University's decision. However, the FSM campaigned for more than free speech. The leader of FSM, **Mario Savio**, was critical of American society as a whole: he said it was like a machine which trapped Americans; the time had come, he declared, to destroy the machine.

In general terms, New Left groups had little support prior to 1965. New Left activists tended to come from wealthy backgrounds and only had a noticeable presence in the elite universities. By October 1963 only six American Universities had SDS groups on campus and the total membership was 610 people. However, the New Left became more influential due to the campaign against the Vietnam War.

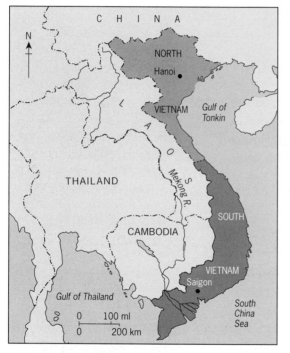

The division of Vietnam.

Take note

As you read through this section identify the two main student groups. Make notes on:
1. their origins and aims
2. their leaders
3. their campaigns.

The anti-war movement: Make Love, Not War

America's involvement in Vietnam, 1945–1975

The USA had been involved in Vietnam, in South East Asia, in one way or another since 1945. Vietnam was divided in two politically. In the North the Viet Cong, Vietnam's Communists, were in control, while in the South a pro-Western government ruled. By 1963 it looked like the Communists were on the brink of winning control of South Vietnam. This presented a problem for the US government, because the President's advisers believed it might create a 'domino effect'. By this they meant that as soon as one of the countries in South East Asia fell to Communism, neighbouring countries would follow. Consequently, in 1965 President Johnson sent 186,000 US troops to fight the Viet Cong. However, the American military was unable to defeat the Communists. As a result, President Johnson committed more soldiers and more money. By 1968, 550,000 Americans were fighting in Vietnam and there was still no sign of victory.

An unpopular war

In 1965 the overwhelming majority of Americans supported military involvement in Vietnam. However, the war became increasingly unpopular for a series of reasons:

- *Deaths:* the American public were horrified at the number of US soldiers who died. More than 11,000 died in 1967; a further 16,500 died in 1968.
- **The Draft:** once a month young men aged 18 to 25 years who were not part of the military were 'called up' and required to join the US army. Many young men did not want to fight and resistance mounted as the death toll rose during the war.
- *An unfair draft:* wealthy white Americans could easily avoid being

drafted into the army by enrolling in colleges and universities. Working-class whites and black Americans found it harder to manipulate the system as they did not have the same access to education. As a result, a disproportionate number of those called up were black or working-class Americans – roughly 80 per cent of soldiers came from poor or working-class families.

- *Low morale:* the war was unpopular with the troops. This is evident from the number of deserters: approximately 20 per cent of new soldiers went absent without leave during the initial training. Low morale is also evident from the amount of drugs used by American soldiers. Around a quarter of US troops used hard drugs such as heroin and a greater proportion used soft drugs such as marijuana.

- *A racist war:* many believed that the Vietnam War was a racial war in which the white American government sought to conquer an Asian country.

- *Tactics:* starting in February 1965, President Johnson ordered heavy air force bombing raids which led to the deaths of thousands of Vietnamese civilians including woman and children.

The anti-war movement

SDS radicals believed that the Vietnam War was clear evidence that the US government was corrupt and that it cared more about money and power than it did about people. Additionally, the war was a very personal issue for students. The majority of the soldiers fighting in the Vietnam War were university-aged students, between 19 and 22 years old. As a result almost all students knew someone who had been killed or injured in the war. Additionally, male university students lived in fear of being drafted into the armed forces in order to fight in Vietnam.

In April 1965 SDS organised the first mass anti-war rally in Washington DC. The protest attracted around 20,000 people. SDS also encouraged students to speak out against the war in their universities and colleges. For example, in 1965 SDS organised a 'teach-in' at the University of Michigan during which lectures were cancelled and staff and students met to debate the war. The teach-in protest spread to campuses across America. Within weeks lectures were suspended at the University of Chicago, University of Pennsylvania and the University of Buffalo and the University of Columbia in New York. Many prominent academics participated in the teach-ins. As a result the anti-war movement gained a degree of respectability.

Following the success of the teach-ins, various anti-war groups came together as the Vietnam Day Committee (VDC) to organise further protests. For example, in November 1965 40,000 descended on Washington, marching from the White House to the Lincoln Memorial demanding an end to the war. The San Francisco Diggers also organised an important anti-war protest known as the 'human be-in', which attracted 30,000 people. The 'be-in' was a joint protest against the Vietnam War and the banning of LSD. Protestors listened to countercultural bands and enjoyed free LSD.

Take note

As you read through this section, make a bullet-pointed list of the causes of the Vietnam War and a spider diagram of the reasons why the Vietnam War was unpopular. Draw lines between the different aspects to show how the different reasons were linked. Write notes on the diagram to make the links clear. For example, you could link the number of deaths to dissatisfaction about the Draft.

Glossary:
The Draft

Technically known as Selective Service, this was a process by which young men between the ages of 18 and 25 years were selected at random and required to serve in the US army.

Take note

Draw a table. The left-hand column should be half the width of the right-hand column.
In the left-hand column write very brief descriptions of the different campaigns, for example you could write 'SDS: rally in Washington'. In the right-hand column write more detailed notes on the nature of the campaign, including the date, the form of the protest, who organised the campaign and the number of people who attended.

Source 17.2:

Marianne DeKoven, a member of SDS, remembers the Vietnam War.

It would be difficult to overestimate the horror of the Vietnam War as a daily fact of campus life in the 1960s. The horror of death, maiming, burning, terror and unthinkable destruction of a small country on the evening news, coupled with the threat of the Draft, made it feel like nothing else, nothing good in life, could have any meaning while the war continued.
Extract from: *Utopia Limited: The Sixties and the Emergence of the Postmodern* by Marianne DeKoven (2004)

Take note

As you read through this section, write a detailed paragraph evaluating the success of the anti-war campaign between 1965 and 1968.

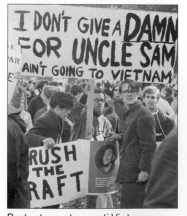

Protestors at an anti-Vietnam War rally hold signs bearing anti-war and anti-draft slogans, Washington D.C., 1967.

Black campaigners played an important part in the anti-war movement. SNCC, for example, were involved in the teach-ins. Martin Luther King also spoke out against the Vietnam War and led a march of 5000 anti-war protestors through Chicago in 1967. The champion boxer and member of the Nation of Islam, Muhammad Ali, refused to fight in the war. He famously told reporters 'I ain't got no quarrel with them Viet Cong ... They never called me nigger.'

Another form of protest was the burning of draft cards. In order to provide enough troops to fight in the war, the government organised a draft of young men. Between 1964 and 1968 300,000 men a year between the ages of 18 and 25 years were drafted. Indeed, by 1968 one-third of 20-year-old men had been called to fight in Vietnam.

The Draft created enormous resentment among young men who did not want to fight in the Vietnam War. Burning draft cards became a symbolic act of resistance against the war. The government responded by criminalising the act. The protestors, in turn, took the government to court, arguing that the new law violated their right to free speech as part of a case known as *United States v. O'Brien*. The Supreme Court ruled that the new law did not take away the right to free speech due to the fact that burning a draft card was not in fact an act of speaking.

The Draft served to radicalise many young men. Consequently, SDS's membership rose from 1500 in 1965 to 30,000 by the spring of 1967.

A final group who opposed the war were the Youth International Party, or Yippies. The group are a good example of the overlap between the counterculture and political activism. Their organisation reflected their rejection of authority, as they had no leader and no hierarchy. Their flag struck a chord with many within the counterculture as it featured a green cannabis leaf. The Yippies helped to organise the anti-war march on the Pentagon in 1967 and put forward a pig as a candidate for the 1968 Presidential election.

The impact of the anti-war movement

In general terms the anti-war movement failed to persuade the American people that the Vietnam War was unjust. As late as 1968, 56 per cent of Americans described themselves as '**hawks**' while only 28 per cent admitted to being '**doves**'. What is more, a significant number of those who did not consider themselves hawks believed that the anti-war protestors were unpatriotic and that all protest undermined the efforts of the American troops who were fighting and dying in Vietnam.

The US government was also unmoved by the anti-war protests. Rather than withdrawing troops, President Johnson's strategy was to commit ever greater numbers of troops to the war. Finally, the anti-war movement failed to persuade the media to criticise the war, at least prior to 1969. Generally, the television networks supported the war effort and refused to broadcast upsetting footage. Between 1965 and 1970 it is estimated that only 76 out of the 2300 television news programmes featured footage of dead or wounded soldiers. Rather, the media criticised the anti-war protestors and tended to label all protestors as radical hippies.

Conclusion

The counterculture that had flowered in the 1960s had largely disappeared by 1970. Some hippie communes were infiltrated by criminals such as **Charles Manson**, who took advantage of the 'anything goes' atmosphere of the 'crash pads'. Equally, hippie communes could not cope with the needs of the young people who turned to the communes in order to escape abuse and problems at home. Sexual liberation also lost its appeal for many women who discovered that sexual liberation often meant sexual exploitation.

Charles Manson

(born 1934)

Notorious leader of a group called 'the Manson Family'. The Family appeared to be a hippie group, but in reality Manson encouraged them to kill and mutilate. In one case the family killed 12 people in one evening.

Glossary:

Hawk

A person who believes in pursuing aggressive foreign policies, such as war, in order to achieve their political aims.

Dove

A person who wishes to avoid war and use peaceful means to resolve international issues.

Activity: The 1960s – a Biography

Biographies normally deal with a single person, but in recent years historians have been using biographies to discuss other things, such as Gerard J. DeGroot's *The Bomb: A Life* (2005), which contains a biography of the atomic bomb.

Imagine you are writing a 'biography' of the 1960s. Drawing on the information in this chapter and your study of civil rights in the 1960s, plan a biography of the 1960s.

Your plan should include:

1. A catchy title, and possibly a subtitle.
2. A one-paragraph summary of your argument – explain what the key themes of the 1960s were and why you believe they are important.
3. A chapter breakdown – your book should contain a series of chapters dealing with the different aspects of the 1960s. For each chapter write one or two sentences outlining what the chapter will deal with.
4. A cover image. Using an Internet image search engine, select a picture that you think represents the 1960s. Write a paragraph explaining why the image is appropriate for the book.

Taking it further

Films are often a good window into the culture of past generations. This is certainly true of the 1960s. Stanley Kubrick's film *2001: A Space Odyssey* (1968), although set in the 21st century, is rooted in the concerns of the 1960s. Watch the film and see if you can spot examples of:

- 1960s optimism
- the 'populuxe' lifestyle
- Cold War tensions with the Soviet Union
- worries about life becoming increasingly artificial
- the influence of psychedelic culture.

Chapter 18 Women's liberation

Key questions

- What issues faced American women in the 1960s?
- What action did feminist groups and the US government take to address these issues?
- How far had sexual equality been achieved by 1968?

In April 1968 female students at the University of Columbia struck a blow for sexual equality. A group of revolutionary students took over the University's central buildings in protest at the suspension of six students who had been anti-war activists. However, once the University had been occupied the male students expected the female students to do the housekeeping chores. The female students refused, claiming that 'feminists don't cook'. Their slogan clearly indicates that feminism is about much more than political or economic rights.

Take note

Draw a table. The left-hand column should be half the width of the right-hand column.

- In the left-hand column write 'First Wave', 'Second Wave' and 'Third Wave'.
- In the right-hand column make notes on the objectives of each wave and the period in which they took place.

Glossary:

Feminism

The term does not have a fixed meaning, but it is often used to describe the belief that women should have political, social, sexual and economic rights equal to those of men.

Timeline

1963	*The Feminine Mystique* published
1967	Executive Order 11375 outlaws sexual discrimination in companies working for the government
	Weeks v. Southern Bell results in first successful prosecution of sexist practice in the workplace
1968	*The Institution of Sexual Intercourse* published
	New York Radical Women (NYRW) protest against the Miss World pageant

Introduction: the issues facing American women in the 1960s

Historians often describe **feminism** as progressing in a series of waves.

- First wave feminism, which ended in 1920, addressed women's political rights.
- Second wave, or liberal, feminism addressed economic issues.
- Third wave, or radical, feminism addressed more fundamental issues such as female identity as well as domestic and sexual relationships.

Women's problems and feminist solutions

Economics

Liberal feminists of the 1960s had three major economic concerns: employment opportunities, income and unpaid work. First, women had very limited opportunities in the workplace. In 1960 there were 23 million women in the workforce compared with just 18 million in 1940. Nonetheless, this still meant that more than three-fifths of women over the age of 16 were not at work. The figure was much lower among some groups of women. For example, only 30 per cent of married mothers had any kind of paid employment in 1960.

Income was another big issue as working women earned 57 per cent of that of working men throughout the 1960s. The average annual income for a man in 1961 was around $27,000; women, on the other hand, earned on average $15,000 a year. Finally, feminists identified the issue of unpaid work such as childcare. During the 1960s women were responsible for 79 per cent of America's unpaid work. Notably, most women with a job were also unpaid family workers. In this sense feminists argued that many women were expected to do a 'double shift.'

In order to address these issues, feminists campaigned for an Equal Rights Act that would outlaw sexual discrimination in terms of hiring and pay.

Identity

Feminists were also troubled by the notion of female identity. Black Power groups argued that black people had been stripped of their identity through slavery. Similarly, radical feminists argued that women's identity had been defined by men. **Betty Friedan's** *The Feminine Mystique* (1963) argued that women's lives and identities had become focused on their husbands and their children. Friedan's solution to this was further education and greater involvement in work, in order to forge a new identity independent of their family.

Some radical feminists advocated more far-reaching solutions. The 'super militant Amazon' Ti-Grace Atkinson, for example, argued that female inequality is rooted in heterosexual relationships. Atkinson's 1968 essay 'The Institution of Sexual Intercourse' argued that all male–female relationships are **patriarchal** and force women to be **submissive**. First, sex between men and women leads to women having babies and this robs them of their chance to participate in society in other ways. Second, Atkinson argued that sex between men and women is always exploitative; that is to say that men gain from it at women's expense. Finally, Atkinson argued that heterosexual sex is often violent and coercive. Indeed, Atkinson was critical of romantic love. She argued that love is a psychological trap set by men to force women into submission. With reference to the Vietnam War she suggested that love was a 'psychological draft' that forced women to enlist in a male-dominated society. In response to these problems, Atkinson advocated celibacy or lesbianism and female separatism. In the long term she envisioned the abolition of sexual intercourse and romantic love. Atkinson's radical message was highly influential in the sense that it promoted the campaign for gay rights in the 1970s.

Government action under Kennedy and Johnson

With the election of President Kennedy in 1960, feminists began lobbying the government again. In response, Kennedy set up the Presidential Commission on the Status of Women, also known as the Kennedy Commission. In addition, the Democratic Congressman Howard W. Smith proposed an amendment to the 1964 Civil Rights Act that would outlaw sexual discrimination as well as racial discrimination.

Take note

Draw the following table.

Problems	Solutions

In the left-hand column make a list of the issues affecting women. In the right-hand column make a note of the solutions proposed by feminists. Make sure you distinguish between 'liberal' and 'radical' solutions.

Betty Friedan

(1921–2006)

Writer, activist and feminist. She is remembered for her book *The Feminine Mystique* (1963) and for her role in the foundation of the National Organization for Women (NOW).

Glossary:

Patriarchal

Related to a social system in which women are dominated by men.

Submissive

Obeying the will of another.

Take note

As you read through this section make a note of:
1. the evidence that governments of the 1960s took women's issues seriously
2. the evidence that they failed to advance women's equality.

Your notes could be in the form of a table, lists or a spider diagram.

Then write a paragraph evaluating the government's success in outlawing sexual discrimination.

Glossary:

Title VII

Many acts have several different clauses or parts which set out different aspects of the law. In American law they are called titles. Title VII of the 1964 Civil Rights Act explicitly outlaws sexual discrimination in employment.

Source 18.1: Activist Sarah Evans recalls how women were treated in SDS.

Women were invisible in SDS. All of the papers for conferences were prepared by men. Hardly any women spoke in meetings or workshops. One woman who chaired a session at the conference was booed and hissed.

Taken from: *Faces of Feminism* by Sheila Tobias (1997)

Nonetheless, the 1964 Civil Rights Act of Johnson's presidency was a hollow victory. The government refused to enforce **Title VII**, the aspect of the Act that protected women. Indeed, the gap in earnings between men and women was wider in 1969 than it had been in 1963. Government inaction spurred women to more radical action and in 1966 some of the original members of the Kennedy Commission formed a new campaigning group: the National Organization for Women (NOW).

The growth of feminism in the 1960s

Feminist movements grew in the USA in the late 1960s for three main reasons.

- As the Student Nonviolent Coordinating Committee (SNCC) and the Congress of Racial Equality (CORE) began to exclude white members, the excluded campaigners turned their attention to other issues.
- Women played a key role in the civil rights movement, particularly at a local level. Black campaigners such as Jo Ann Robinson and Fannie Lou Hamer inspired women to become politically active.
- The New Left, the anti-war movement and particularly Students for a Democratic Society (SDS) were male-dominated. One disenchanted member summed up SDS by saying 'men made the decisions while women made the coffee'. As a result, radical white women began to organise new groups focusing on women's rights.

Feminists, much like campaigners for black rights, were often divided in terms of their goals and their methods. In general terms feminist activism in the 1960s reflected the division between second wave and radical feminists.

NOW: Campaigning for equal rights

The National Organization for Women (NOW), America's biggest feminist group, was founded in 1966 by Betty Friedan. Friedan and Rev **Pauli Murray** set out NOW's aims in the NOW Statement of Purpose. Essentially, NOW's aim was to 'to bring women into full participation in the mainstream of American society... in a truly equal partnership with men'. In order to achieve this NOW campaigned for an Equal Rights Amendment – a change to the American Constitution guaranteeing equal rights to men and women.

NOW's preliminary campaigns focused on employment. The group's initial tactic was lobbying President Johnson's government. The leading figures in NOW were well connected due to their involvement in the Kennedy Commission. Consequently, by mid-1967 NOW had chalked up a series of legal victories.

- In May President Johnson signed Executive Order 11375 outlawing sexual discrimination in any company that worked for the government.
- The Equal Employment Opportunity Commission (EEOC) held a test case showing that it was now willing to enforce Title VII of the Civil Rights Act.
- Finally, Johnson promised to appoint 50 women to top government posts and asked NOW to advise him on the appointments.

Feminists march in New York City, 26 August 1970, to mark the 50th anniversary of American women being given the right to vote. The National Organization for Women (NOW) called upon all American women to strike for equality on that day.

NOW also used the courts. The 1967 case *Weeks v. Southern Bell* is typical of the cases NOW was involved with. Lorena Weeks had taken the Southern Bell Telephone Company to court for promoting a man in spite of the fact that she was better qualified and had more experience. Weeks lost the first round of her case but Sylvia Roberts, NOW's chief lawyer in Louisiana, took on the case when it went to appeal. Weeks faced enormous obstacles: the management at Southern Bell made her life very difficult and her husband and children were embarrassed by her high profile campaign. In spite of these obstacles, NOW's legal team triumphed. The court ruled that Southern Bell had violated Title VII of the Civil Rights Act. Weeks won the job and $31,000 in back pay. Southern Bell tried a series of delaying tactics, but in 1971 Weeks finally got justice. The Weeks case set a **precedent**, opening the way for other women to challenge sexist practice in the workplace.

NOW also addressed inequalities in criminal law. In 1966 Jane Daniel was convicted of robbery. She received a longer sentence than her male accomplice due to Pennsylvania's Muncy Act which stated that women should receive longer sentences than men. NOW showed that this Act violated Title VII and the Muncy Act was struck down by Pennsylvania's highest court.

Radical feminists: Campaigning for women's liberation

Many radical feminists were originally members of NOW and split away due to their belief that NOW was not radical enough. For example, **Kate Millet** left NOW due to its unwillingness to campaign for lesbian rights. Atkinson also left NOW to form a New York-based group called The Feminists. Atkinson's new group excluded men and married women from membership. The Feminists campaigned against pornography and marriage and in favour of abortion on demand. In one of their anti-marriage campaigns The Feminists stormed the New York City registry office armed with leaflets advocating female separatism.

The New York Radical Women (NYRW), another third wave feminist group, organised women's 'speakouts'. For example, NYRW organised events where women would 'speakout' about their abortions. The public meetings proved

Take note

Draw the following table:

As you read through this section:

- list the areas of sexual inequality in the first column
- make detailed notes on NOW's campaigns in the second column
- in the third column make notes on the successes or failures of NOW's campaigns.

Having completed this table, write a paragraph evaluating the success of NOW's campaigns in the 1960s.

Sexual inequalities	NOW's campaigns	Successes or failures

Pauli Murray

(1910–1985)

Pauli Murray was described as a 'one-woman civil rights movement' due to her dynamic activism for equal rights in America. She was involved in the *Brown v. Board of Education* case of 1954, and in 1961 she was appointed to the Presidential Commission on the Status of Women (see page 105).

Glossary:

Precedent

Legal case establishing a principle that will become the basis of future court decisions.

Take note

Draw the following table.
As you read this section:

- list the areas of inequality in the first column
- make detailed notes on the different radical feminist campaigns in the second column
- in the third column make notes on the successes or failures of campaigns.

Then write a paragraph comparing the successes and failures of NOW's campaigns with those of the campaigns of the more radical feminists.

Sexual inequalities	Radical feminist campaigns	Successes or failures

Kate Millet

(born 1934)

Radical feminist writer, best known for her 1970 book *Sexual Politics*. In the 1970s she moved to Iran to campaign for women's rights, but was soon deported.

Glossary:
Sex object

A person no longer viewed as a human being seen as an object whose purpose is the sexual pleasure of another.

Taking it further

Complete the following essay. How successful were American feminists in the period 1963–1969?

to be very powerful and encouraged many to rethink their perspective on America's restrictive abortion laws. NYRW also organised a famous protest against the Miss World pageant in 1968. The NYRW believed the pageant turned women into **sex objects**. The NYRW protest involved crowning a sheep Miss World and throwing their underwear, kitchen utensils and other symbols of male oppression into a 'freedom trash-can'.

> ### Source 18.2: An excerpt from The Feminists' manifesto.
>
> We seek the self-development of every individual woman. To accomplish this we must eliminate the institutions which enforce the female role. We must destroy love because it promotes vulnerability, dependence, possessiveness, and prevents the full development of woman's human potential by directing all her energies to the interests of others.
> Taken from: *Radical Feminism* by Koedt et al. (1973)

How successful were women's groups in the 1960s?

The women's movements of the 1960s enjoyed some successes. Title VII of the Civil Rights Act and Executive Order 11375 established the legal foundation for sexual equality in the workplace. Moreover, legal campaigns such as *Weeks v. Southern Bell* showed that the law could be used to ensure justice for women. However, NOW's campaigns never led to the passing of an Equal Rights Amendment. It should also be noted that neither Title VII nor Executive Order 11375 resulted in better status or pay for women in the 1960s.

Radical feminists had more limited successes. NYRW's pro-abortion campaigns did not lead to any legal relaxation in abortion laws. Indeed, in 1970 New York State tightened its abortion laws. In 1973 America's abortion laws were relaxed due to *Roe v. Wade,* a more traditional legal campaign. Female separatism also proved unattractive to the majority of women and therefore impossible to achieve.

Activity: **Press conferences**

Press conferences were an important part of radical campaigning in the 1960s as they allowed radicals to get their message into the public domain.

Take on the role of one of the women's groups in this chapter and organise a press conference. Your group should make a brief statement outlining: the issues facing women; your suggestions for change; criticisms of other women's groups; the launch of a new campaign. Use information from this chapter. You should also be prepared to answer questions from journalists.

As well as taking on the role of a women's group, you should also take a turn as a journalist at another group's conference, so prepare some good questions! Finally, as a journalist, write a press report outlining the aims of the group you interviewed, describing their campaign and offering any criticisms you feel are justified.

Chapter 19 Challenging racism outside the black community: Native Americans and Hispanic Americans

Key questions

- What were the problems facing Native Americans and Hispanic Americans in the 1960s?
- In what ways did Native Americans and Hispanic Americans campaign to improve their position?
- How far had the position of Native Americans and Hispanic Americans improved by 1968?

In 1968 America achieved an important first in the space race between the USA and Soviet Union. The spaceship Apollo 8 took a three-man crew to the Moon. The men on board were the first people in human history to be far enough away to see the whole of the Earth. They reported back that they saw one world, not a world divided between North and South or black and white. They saw one world shared by one human race. In spite of this vision, America remained divided. Indeed, in the late 1960s racial protests broadened to include campaigns on behalf of Hispanic Americans and Native Americans.

Timeline

1944	National Congress of American Indians (NCAI) established
1952	Cesar Chávez joins the Community Service Organisation (CSO)
1953	Congressional Resolution 108 – beginning of the legal policy of termination
1960	National Indian Youth Council (NIYC) established
	Mexican American Political Association founded
1962	Chávez leaves the CSO to form the National Farm Workers Association (NFWA)
	Edward Roybal elected to the House of Representatives
1965	Beginning of *La Huelga (The Strike)* – the Delano grape strike
1966	*Peregrinacion* – Pilgrimage of protest
	Government informally ends the policy of termination
1967	Indian Resources Development Act
	Young Chicanos for Community Action (YCCA) established
1968	Table Grape Boycott begins
	Chicano Blowouts
1970	The Delano grape strike and the Table Grape Boycott ends
1975	California Agricultural Labor Relations Act passed

Take note

Make a table with four headings:

- General problems facing Hispanic Americans
- Specific examples of these problems
- Campaigns designed to solve these problems
- Effectiveness of these campaigns

Use the information in this chapter to fill it in.

Introduction

Black people were not the only racial minority that suffered in America. Hispanic Americans and Native Americans also faced discrimination and

Glossary:

Hispanic Americans

A term describing all Americans of Spanish decent. It can also be used to describe all Americans who speak Spanish as their first language.

Chicano

A term describing Mexican Americans; a shortened version of the word 'Mexicano'. Originally, like the word 'black', Chicano was used as a term of abuse, but campaigners in the 1960s used the word positively to describe themselves.

Poverty

According to the American government, anyone who earned less than $3,100 lived in poverty in 1960.

César Chávez

(1927–1993)

Chicano leader of the Community Service Organisation (CSO), National Farm Workers Association (NFWA) and later the United Farm Workers (UFW). He was a shy man, a vegan and a Roman Catholic. He worked as an agricultural labourer for most of his life before turning to political activism. He was inspired by Martin Luther King and Gandhi and advocated non-violent direct action.

poverty. Inspired by black activists, radicals from both communities became organised during the 1960s in order to fight for a fairer America.

Hispanic Americans

The problems facing Hispanic Americans

Many **Hispanic Americans** worked in the Californian farming industry. By 1965 'agribusiness' in California was worth over $4 billion and generated 43 per cent of the fruit and vegetables sold in America. **Chicano** workers were only employed seasonally during the harvests. Consequently, Chicanos in California worked an average of 134 days a year, often migrating across California harvesting one crop after another.

The lack of full-time employment and low wages meant that Californian Chicanos lived in extreme **poverty**. The average annual income for Chicanos in California was just $1,378. They lived in low quality rented accommodation or makeshift farm camps with very basic facilities. Chicano families accounted for 80 per cent of Californian welfare cases.

Many white Californians assumed that Chicanos earned little because they were lazy. However, in reality Chicano families worked exceptionally hard harvesting in the fields during daylight hours and then fishing or hunting in the evenings to feed their families. One of the reasons for the poverty of the Chicanos was the fact that farming unions had no legal protection and as a result it was difficult for the labourers to organise and fight injustice.

César Chávez

César Chávez was the leading campaigner for Chicano rights. His family were so poor that he did not have shoes and they were forced to live in tents or very basic rented accommodation, and on some occasions in the family's car.

Chávez was brought up a Roman Catholic. Like Martin Luther King, Chávez's Christian faith led him to renounce violence while at the same time inspiring him to fight injustice. In 1952 he joined the Community Service Organisation (CSO) which fought for Chicano rights. Chávez's commitment and hard work led to promotions and by 1962 he was national director of the CSO. Nonetheless, the CSO were not willing to organise Chicano workers into a labour union and for this reason Chávez resigned from the CSO in 1962 and set up the National Farm Workers Association (NFWA).

National Farm Workers Association

Chávez's strategy for the NFWA had two parts. Initially, he hoped to establish a union that would provide welfare support for Chicano workers. However, once the union grew he hoped to organise a national campaign to gain greater economic rights for Chicano farm workers.

Following its foundation in 1962 the NFWA provided a series of services to its members. For example, the NFWA set up a credit union which allowed Chicano workers to borrow money. It also established an insurance scheme. Both of these initiatives were extremely useful as traditional banks and insurance firms had no interest in providing services to people living below the poverty line. The NFWA also had advisors who would help families deal with local authorities in order to ensure they were treated fairly. These schemes were popular, and as a result membership of the NFWA grew from 200 in 1962 to more than 1200 in 1965.

La Huelga!

The NFWA launched its first big campaign in 1965. Filipino farm workers, led by the Agricultural Workers Organizing Committee (AWOC), walked out of the vineyards in Delano, California, starting a strike on 8 September 1965. Eight days later the NFWA voted to support the strike. This marked the beginning of *La Huelga* – The Strike, which lasted five years and involved over 10,000 farm workers. Agricultural firms refused to negotiate with the strikers. Rather, farming bosses attempted to break the strike by evicting farm workers from their camps on the farms and recruiting **strike breakers**.

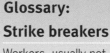

Glossary:
Strike breakers

Workers, usually not members of unions, who are hired to replace workers who are on strike.

In order to help organise the strike the NFWA and AWOC merged creating the United Farm Workers (UFW). Members of this union were often known as *Chavistas* after Chávez, their leader.

Chávez's strategy, like that of black civil rights leaders, was to attract media attention and in so doing expose the appalling conditions that Chicano and Filipino workers were forced to endure. First, he organised the *Peregrinacion*, or Pilgrimage – a 340-mile march from the vineyards to the offices of the Governor of California. Second, Chávez fasted for 25 days from February to March 1968. **Robert F. Kennedy**, who was campaigning to become the next American President, met with Chávez during the fast and publically supported the UFW's struggle. Finally, in 1968 UFW spearheaded a boycott of Californian grapes. The Table Grape Boycott was extraordinarily successful. It lasted until 1970 and at its height 17 million Americans stopped buying Californian grapes.

César Chávez pickets outside a Californian Safeway, 1973.

The UFW's achievements

The strikes and boycotts were effective, but they took time. The first success came in 1966 when the Schenley Vineyards negotiated a fair contract with farm workers. By 1970 the UFW's activism had forced the Delano grape producers to introduce a wage increase, bringing the worker's pay up to the level of the national minimum wage. As a result the grape strike and the boycott came to an end. The largest victory for the strikers was the passage of the California Agricultural Labor Relations Act in 1975. This gave agricultural unions legal rights and agricultural firms were required to negotiate with them by law.

Robert F. Kennedy

(1925–1968)

Younger brother of John F. Kennedy. Robert Kennedy was Attorney General from 1961 to 1964 and a US Senator from 1965 until his assassination in 1968.

Other Hispanic American protest

Not all Hispanic Americans were engaged in agriculture. Consequently, protest groups were formed to address further political and social issues facing Chicanos in American cities. In 1960, the Mexican American

Take note

Produce a table in four columns using the following headings:
1. General problems facing Native Americans
2. Specific examples of these problems
3. Campaigns designed to solve these problems
4. Effectiveness of these campaigns

Use the information in the rest of the chapter to complete all four columns.

Glossary:
Native Americans

One of a number of terms that describe the indigenous people of North America. There is still no agreed term and therefore they are known by a variety of different names such as 'Native American', 'American Indian' and 'Amerindian'. Notably, the term 'Red Indian' is no longer in use.

Reservations

Territories within North America that serve as homelands for Native American tribes. There are 314 reservations which total 44 million acres. The reservations are self-governing. The reservation land cannot be sold by the tribes who live on it without the permission of the Bureau of Indian Affairs.

Political Association (MAPA) was created to encourage Mexican Americans to register to vote, and to support Mexican Americans running for public office. In 1962, MAPA President, Edward Roybal, was elected to the House of Representatives. Additionally, in the later 1960s, a youth organisation, Young Chicanos for Community Action (YCCA), was established. Heavily influenced by the Black Panthers, this organisation campaigned for better education and employment practices for Chicanos in Los Angeles. Notably, they were involved in the Chicano Blowouts of 1968, a series of school walkouts demanding a higher standard of schooling for Hispanic students. There were also Hispanic American communities in other big American cities, such as Puerto Rican communities who lived in the ghettos of New York and Chicago. They faced racial discrimination in terms of housing and employment similar to that experienced by the black communities of those cities.

Hispanic American protest borrowed aims and methods from the civil rights movement. However, it never achieved the publicity or success of the black protestors. This was for three reasons:

- Hispanic Americans formed only 6 per cent of the American population, while the black population of American stood at 12 per cent of the total population.
- The federal government was less sympathetic towards Hispanic Americans. Their lower numbers – coupled with low levels of voter registration – meant that they had less voting power than the black population, and therefore less political influence.
- The Hispanic American movement was fragmented. Mexican Americans, Cuban Americans and Puerto Ricans were all labelled 'Hispanic', but in reality the groups were divided on political and cultural lines.

Native Americans

The Native American population

In 1960 there were 523,591 **Native Americans** living in America. Over one-half of these lived in rural areas, a much higher proportion than that of the population in general. Approximately 25 per cent lived on **reservations**. The largest Native American populations were located in Oklahoma, California, Arizona and New Mexico. Native American communities were organised into tribes. The largest tribes were the Cherokee, the Navajo, the Chippewa and the Sioux, with each tribe having its own culture.

Native American politics

The right of Native American tribes to govern themselves had been recognised by the American government in the nineteenth century. Prior to this, white settlers had waged war on them. Indeed, as result of war and disease the Native American people were almost wiped out. The self-governing tribes had their own police forces, law courts and tribal councils. Nonetheless, the reservations were managed by the **Bureau of Indian Affairs** (BIA), a part of the American federal government. Relations between the BIA and the tribal leaders were often tense – both sides blamed each other for the problems within the community.

Economic and social problems

Native Americans did not enjoy the fruits of the post-war economic boom. For example, unemployment on Native American reservations was sometimes as high as 70 per cent during the 1960s. Of the 32,000 Native Americans on Navajo reservations in 1965, only 8000 had a job which paid a regular wage. Native American life was also plagued by social problems such as alcoholism. For example, 84 per cent of arrests made on Navajo reservations in 1960 were alcohol-related.

The 1964 Civil Rights Act contained measures which addressed some of the economic and social problems that affected Native Americans. For example, the Act outlawed racial discrimination within employment. Consequently, Native Americans gained a legally-defensible right to be treated fairly in the workplace. President Johnson's Education Act of 1965 also catered for Native Americans by establishing the National Advisory Council on Indian Education in order to increase literacy rates among Native Americans. Further to this, in 1968, Johnson founded the National Council on Indian Opportunity. The Council had a budget of $400 million and was charged with tackling problems such as alcoholism, discrimination in health services and raising the standard of vocational training available to Native Americans. Finally, the 1968 Civil Rights Act outlawed discrimination against Native Americans in the housing market.

Native American activists and campaigns

There were two main campaign groups representing Native Americans in the 1960s: the National Congress of American Indians (NCAI) and the National Indian Youth Council (NIYC). Both were **pan-Indian** groups – that is to say, they tried to represent all Native Americans rather than individual tribes.

The Eisenhower government of the 1950s had pursued a policy of 'termination' in an attempt to solve the problems of Native Americans. Termination meant ending the special legal status of the Native American tribes. For example, Congressional Resolution 108 of August 1953 returned reservation land to the control of local governments in California, Minnesota, Nebraska, Oregon and Wisconsin. The policy was designed to force Native Americans to become part of mainstream American culture in the hope that integration would solve their problems.

The NCAI, established in 1944, fought against this policy. Its main tactic was lobbying the government. The NCAI also collaborated with Professor **Sol Tax** at the University of Chicago to organise the 1961 American Indian Chicago Conference. The Conference published the *Declaration of Indian Purpose,* which set out an alternative policy to termination. Essentially, it proposed reversing the policy and devolving power from central government to local tribal leaders.

In general terms the Chicago Conference proved to be highly influential. Dr Philleo Nash, appointed by President Kennedy to be head of the BIA in 1961, worked closely with Native American leaders to ensure that

Glossary:
Bureau of Indian Affairs

The part of the American federal government tasked with managing the land which forms the Native American reservations.

Glossary:
Pan-Indian

Representing all Native Americans rather than individual tribes.

Sol Tax

(1907–1995)

A Professor at the University of Chicago who specialised in Native American cultures. He was involved in the 1960s counterculture, campaigning for Native American rights and opposing the Vietnam War.

government reforms led to an improvement of life on the reserves. He ensured that 56 reservations were turned into 'Redevelopment Areas' – areas which would receive government funding and assistance in using this funding.

Second, President Lyndon B. Johnson initiated the Indian Resources Development Act of 1967 which allowed Native American tribes to sell and mortgage their land and in so doing raise financial resources for their communities. Both of these policies went hand-in-hand with an attempt on the part of the federal government to pass the administration of these projects to local Native American leaders. Additionally, in 1966 the policy of compulsory termination was unofficially abandoned.

The National Indian Youth Council (NIYC), established in 1960, also campaigned against termination. By the late 1960s, influenced by groups such as the Black Panthers, NIYC had adopted a position of 'red nationalism' or 'red power'. Their nationalism stressed the need for self-determination: an extension of Native American rights over the reservations. The phrase 'self-determination' was adopted by government policymakers to describe the NIYC's approach to Native American rights in the late 1960s. The 'red nationalism' of the NIYC had an important effect on later campaigns at the end of the 1960s and throughout the 1970s. For example, in 1969 a group of red nationalists called Indians of All Tribes (IAT) occupied the disused prison on the Island of Alcatraz, demanding that the island be returned to the Native American people. Although the campaign did not succeed in returning Alcatraz to Native American control, President Richard Nixon officially announced the end of the policy of termination during the occupation.

Conclusion

Black activists were extremely influential during the 1960s. Inspired by Martin Luther King, César Chávez used nonviolent direct action and economic boycotts to fight for a better deal for Chicano farm workers. Inspired by black student radicals, the National Indian Youth Council (NIYC) fought for red power and red nationalism. The National Congress of American Indians (NCAI) also played its part in saving the Indian Tribes and forcing the government to abandon the policy of termination.

Taking it further

Throughout this course you have studied many forms of protest. For example, you have studied boycotts, strikes, marches and armed self-defence groups. Reach a judgement about which form of protest was most effective in the period 1945–1968. Write a paragraph explaining your choice. Make sure that you support your conclusions with at least one specific example.

Activity: Comparing campaigns

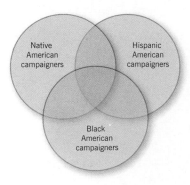

You have now studied how three racial groups in America (Black Americans, Hispanic Americans and Native Americans) campaigned for greater rights. For each group, make a list of the aims of the campaigners and the methods used by the campaigners.

Copy the Venn diagram onto a large sheet of paper.

Use your lists to complete the diagram, showing the extent to which the aims and methods of these groups overlapped. You may wish to use one colour to represent the aims and a second colour to represent the methods.

Discuss as a class: how far were the aims and methods of Hispanic American and Native American campaign groups influenced by those of the civil rights movement?

Skills Builder 4: **Extended writing**

So far, in the Skills Builders, you have learned about:

- the importance of writing in paragraphs
- answering questions on causation and change
- how to write introductions and conclusions.

Now you are going to learn how to write a full response to an examination question. Remember, you will only have 40 minutes for each answer so you need to make the most of your time.

Read the QUESTION PAPER thoroughly

You will have a choice of two questions on this topic, but you only need to answer one. Make sure you make the right choice. Don't rush, and give yourself a few minutes to decide which question to answer. You won't have time to change your mind halfway through the exam.

Read YOUR CHOSEN QUESTION thoroughly

Once you have made your choice, examine the question and work out what you are expected to do.

What is the question asking you to do?

There are a number of different types of questions you could be asked. Examples are:

- How far...
- How important...
- How extensive...
- To what extent...
- Why...

Make sure that your answer is relevant to the type of question that has been asked: in the first four question types you will be expected to assess a range of factors, weigh up their importance and reach a judgement concerning the question set. For example:

> (A) How far was the economic boom of the 1960s responsible for the emergence of the counterculture?

In answering this question you will be expected to provide evidence of how the economic boom of the 1960s was an important factor in the emergence of the counterculture. You will also be expected to assess the importance of other factors such as the conformity of 1950s and 1960s mainstream culture, the inspiration of black civil rights protests and the development of youth culture.

Make sure you cover the whole question

Here is an example question:

> (B) How successful was the civil rights movement in the period 1957 to 1968?

In this question you must make sure that you cover the entire period 1957 to 1968 and only that period. Notably, answers which deal extensively with periods outside the one set in the question will not do well.

Make a plan

Once you are clear about what the question is asking, sketch out what you are going to cover. Your plan could be a bullet-pointed list or a spider diagram.

Writing the answer

Make sure that you:

- Write a brief introduction, setting out your argument and what you will be discussing in your answer.

- Write a separate paragraph for each of the factors or reasons that you discuss. In each paragraph, make sure that you make a clear point and support it with specific examples.

- At the end of each paragraph make a clear link between the point you have made and the question, showing how the point answers the question.

- Avoid just writing descriptions.

- Avoid merely 'telling the story'.

- Write a concluding paragraph which sums up your argument and provides a clear judgement on the question.

Pace yourself

Success in an examination is based partly on effective time management. If you have approximately 40 minutes to answer a question, make sure you have reached the halfway point after 20 minutes. And after 35 minutes you should start thinking about and then writing your conclusion.

If you run short of time, make sure that you still write a proper conclusion. If necessary, you can save time by cutting short your treatment of the paragraph or paragraphs before, by:

- writing the first sentence containing your point
- bullet-pointing your evidence – the information that backs it up
- writing the last sentence of the paragraph which explains the link between your point and the question.

Read the question paper thoroughly

Be clear about the focus of the question you have chosen

Timing: pace yourself

Make a brief plan of your answer before you start writing

Activity: Write your own answer

Now write your own answer to this question, following the guidance given above:

(C) How widespread was the protest culture of the 1960s?

Examzone

Now that you have finished the course content, you will have to do the last bits of preparation for the exam itself. This advice covers two important elements for exam success: revising the information and using your information well in the examination.

This topic – 'Pursuing Life and Liberty: Equality in the USA, 1945–1968'– is part of Edexcel's Option D: A World Divided: Communism and Democracy in the 20th Century, in Unit 1. The Unit 1 exam will be 1 hour and 20 minutes in length, and is worth 60 marks in total.

In the exam you will be given the choice of two questions on the topic Pursuing Life and Liberty. You will be expected to answer one of these and should spend no more than half the examination time answering it. You will also have to answer another question from a different topic. You will be expected to answer the questions you choose in essay form.

What to expect

You will need to remember information, but the exam is mainly testing whether or not you can apply the relevant information in answering a question. You will be assessed on your ability to recall and select historical knowledge and to deploy it (i.e. make use of knowledge to support your points). You can see that it's not just knowing what happened which counts, but understanding how to use what you know.

You will also be assessed on your ability to present historical explanations that show an understanding of history. You should read the question carefully to make sure you answer it in the right way. Sometimes questions will simply begin 'Why'. These are asking you to analyse the causes of an event or development. For the highest marks you will need to show how factors combined to bring about the event.

Most questions will ask you for a judgement. Here are some different types of question stems you may come across in the exam:

1 How far was x responsible for y?
2 To what extent did x change?
3 How far did x depend on y?
4 Did x play a major part in y?

Although judgement questions come in a variety of forms, they are all asking you to balance points. In the case of example 2 below, you will be looking for evidence of change and of continuity in order to reach a judgement about the extent of change.

When you choose your question in the examination, take note of what sort of judgement it asks you to make. The essay questions test a variety of skills. Here are some examples of different skills being tested by the questions.

- The analysis of, and judgement about, the **key features** of a situation.
  For example: *To what extent is it accurate to claim that violence was the central feature of the Black Power movement?*
- The analysis of, and judgement about, the extent of **change.**
  For example: *How far do you agree that racial equality had been achieved for Hispanic and Native Americans by 1968?*
- The analysis of **consequences** or **effects**.
  For example: *How accurate is it to say that the American Government did nothing to advance racial equality in the period 1945–1957?*
- The analysis of, and judgement about, the **causes** of a historical event or situation.
  For example: *How far were disagreements between Martin Luther King and President Johnson the major reason for the failure of King's northern campaigns?*

Another type of question will ask you how far you agree with a statement. This is still a judgement question. You should clarify what the statement is about so that you know what the question expects of you:

- Is it a statement about causation, like this question: *How far do you agree that Kennedy's death was the main reason for the passing of the 1964 Civil Rights Act?*
- Or is it about change, like this question: *How far do you agree that Martin Luther King transformed the methods used by the civil rights protestors?*

When you are clear about what the question wants from you, you can use what you have learned in the Skills Builder sections of this book to produce an answer based on extended writing (an essay) which will help you to gain high marks.

How to revise

Make a revision plan

Before you start revising, make a plan. Otherwise it is easy to waste your precious revision time. It is helpful to look at your exam dates and work backwards to the first date you intend to start revising. Here are some tips on how to create a revision plan:

1. First, fill in the dates of your examinations and then any regular commitments you have. This will help give you a realistic idea of how much time you have to revise.

2. Plan your time carefully, assigning more time to topics you find difficult.

3. Use a revision 'checklist'. Look at what you need to know and try to identify any gaps in your knowledge.

4. Now fill in the timetable with sensible work slots and breaks.

5. Keep to this timetable! Organise yourself well and it will help you to fulfil your potential. If you have not prepared a revision plan yet, it is not too late to start. Put your plan up somewhere visible so you can refer back to it.

Revision tips

- Revise often – try to do a little every day.

- Make sure you have one day a week when you don't do revision or even think about exams – you'll come back to it refreshed.

- Take a 5- or 10-minute break every hour, and do some stretching exercises, go for a short walk or make a drink.

- Talk to your family or a friend about your revision – they may be able to help you. For example, they could test you on key facts.

- Keep bullet points on 'crib cards' highlighting important revision points. For example, you could have a list or a mind map of the reasons why the Civil Rights Act of 1964 was passed. Use these for quick revision and for reading during 'dead' times – when you're waiting for a bus, for example.

- Use mnemonics. This is when you take the first letter of a series of words you want to remember and then make a new sentence. A common mnemonic for remembering the order of the points of the compass (North, East, South, and West) is 'Naughty Elephants Squirt Water'. You could use a mnemonic to help you remember the US presidents from this period.

- Some people revise well by listening, so you could try 'talking' your revision and recording it onto an mp3 player if you have one. Listen to the recordings while lying in bed, while travelling in a car or walking to the shops. This also takes the guilt out of being out and about rather than in front of your books!

- Practise your exam techniques. As you revise key topics, plan 5 or 6 points to make about the causes/ consequences/ key features / changes relating to major developments. You could use question stems 1–4 on the previous page, and slot in your own x and y.

- Try doing some timed essays. This will make it easier to write a good essay when it comes to the exam.

- Don't panic. Think about what you can achieve, not what you can't. Positive thinking is important! Remember the examiner will be looking to reward you for what you can do.

Assessment Objectives

To do well in your exam, you need to make sure you meet all the assessment objectives. Below are the assessment objectives you need to meet and some advice on how to make sure you meet them.

Recall, select and deploy historical knowledge
AO1a

In your essay, you must show that you can remember, choose and use historical knowledge.

- Remember – *recollect historical facts from your study of this unit*
- Choose – *select specific facts that are relevant to the essay you are writing*
- Use – *place these facts in your essay in a way that supports your argument*

Understanding of the past
AO1b (i)

You need to show that you understand the period studied. Simply telling the story of what happened will not help you to do this. Instead, you need to:

- Analyse – *break down the topic you are considering into key points*
- Explain – *suggest reasons why these key points provide an answer to the question*
- Reach a judgement – *Decide which of your key points was most important and provide reasons to support this*

As you think about analysis, explanation and judgement, remember to bear in mind the relevant **key concepts** and **relationships**.

Key concepts
AO1b (ii)

When faced with an essay question, consider which of the following key concepts it focuses on:

- Causation – *what made an event happen?*
- Consequence – *what were the results of this event?*
- Continuity – *in what ways did things stay the same?*
- Change – *in what ways were things different?*
- Significance – *why was this important?*

Then ensure that your answer remains focused on this concept.

Relationships
AO1b (iii)

Once you have planned the key points you will make in your essay, consider the following:

- How do these key points link together?
- Which key point was most important? Why?

Once you have considered these issues, arrange your points in an order that reflects the way they link together or the relative importance of each key point.

Level descriptors

Each essay you write in the exam will be given a mark out of 30 and will correspond to a level from 1 to 5, with level 5 being the highest. Here is some information about what the levels mean. Read it carefully and use this information to aim for the top!

Level 1:

- General points about the historical period that are correct but not necessarily focused on the topic raised by the question
- The general points will not be supported by accurate and relevant specific examples.

Answers at this level will be very simplistic, irrelevant or vague.

Level 2:

- A number of general points about the topic of the question
- The general points will be supported by some accurate and relevant examples.

Answers at this level might tell the story or part of the story without addressing the question, or might list the key points without backing them up with specific examples.

Level 3:

- A number of points with some focus on the question
- The points will be supported by accurate material, but some whole paragraphs may be either only partly relevant, lacking in detail or both.

At level 3 answers will attempt to focus on the question and have some strengths (some paragraphs will have point, supporting evidence and linkage back to the question), but answers will also have significant areas of weakness. For example, the focus on the question may drift, the answer may lack specific examples or parts of the essay may simply tell the story.

Level 4:

- A number of points which clearly address the question and show an understanding of the most important factors involved
- The points will be supported by accurate material which will be mostly relevant and detailed
- There will be clear explanation of how the points and specific examples provide an answer to the question.

At level 4 answers will clearly attempt to tackle the question and demonstrate a detailed knowledge of the period studied.

Level 5:

- A number of points which clearly address the question and show a thorough understanding of the most important factors involved
- The points will be supported by accurate material which will be relevant and detailed
- There will be clear explanation of how the points and specific examples provide an answer to the question, as well as an evaluation of the relative importance of the different factors or issues discussed.

Answers that are judged to be level 5 will be thorough and detailed – they will clearly engage with the specific question providing a balanced and carefully reasoned argument that reaches a clear and supported judgement.

Sample answer 1

How far had equality for black Americans been achieved by 1968?

An answer given a mark in Level 5 of the published mark scheme

By 1968, significant progress towards equality had been made in the areas of education, transport, public places, voting rights, employment and housing. However, persistent racism meant that black Americans continued to face discrimination in almost all aspects of life. In general there had been substantial de jure progress but de facto change was less significant.

EXAMINER COMMENT

This introduction is focused clearly on the topic. It lists the factors that will be considered and indicates that the essay will provide a balanced answer to the question.

There was a significant move towards equality in the field of education. A number of court cases, starting with Brown v. Board of Education in 1954, established the need for schools to desegregate and went some way towards imposing a timeframe for this desegregation. Further to this, the Civil Rights Act of 1964 gave the federal government the power to challenge segregation. Nonetheless, by the end of 1964, 58 per cent of black schoolchildren remained in segregated schools. President Johnson provided additional economic support for black students through his Higher Education Act of 1965. This provided funding to support the poorest students (many of whom were black) through college. This was highly successful, leading to a fourfold increase in the number of black students in colleges and universities by 1972. In spite of this, education in urban areas was still poor for black children and this is clear from the SNCC's and the Black Panthers' initiatives which targeted education in the late 1960s, such as the Freedom Schools. Overall, by 1968 a great deal of progress had been made towards achieving racial equality in education. The federal government had not only put measures in place to enforce desegregation but had also sought to prevent economic inequalities from preventing black students having access to education.

EXAMINER COMMENT

The first sentence of this paragraph provides a direct link to the question. The supporting evidence is relevant, detailed and wide ranging. The final sentences provide a 'mini-conclusion' to the paragraph, reaching a judgement about the level of equality in education.

There was also progress in terms of desegregation more generally. For example, Morgan v. Virginia (1946) and Browder v. Gayle (1956) established that segregation was illegal on transport between and within states. Furthermore, Boynton v. Virginia (1960) ruled that transport facilities also had to be desegregated. The Freedom Rides of 1961 revealed the extent of opposition to these rulings, but also showed that the federal government was willing to step in to defend them. In this way, by 1968 there was no legal basis for segregation on transport facilities and the federal government had set a precedent for ensuring that desegregation in this respect was enforced.

EXAMINER COMMENT

This paragraph maintains the focus on the extent to which racial equality had been achieved.

The desegregation of public places was another important move towards racial equality. The sit-ins movement that began in 1960 challenged segregation in public places, and by the end of 1963, 161 southern cities had desegregated their restaurants. Following the 1964 Civil Rights Act, the federal government was able to enforce desegregation throughout the South, and by 1965 a total of 214 southern cities had desegregated. However, throughout this period resistance to this form of integration remained high. For example, following the Albany Campaign of 1961-1962, the authorities in Albany closed parks and swimming pools rather than open them to black people.

EXAMINER COMMENT

Again, this paragraph is focused and contains detailed supporting information. However, it does not reach a judgement about how far racial equality had been achieved in public places. A stronger paragraph would conclude with a clear and evaluative link back to the question.

Changes in voting rights signalled substantial progress in terms of racial equality. Eisenhower's Civil Rights Acts of 1957 and 1960 had only a limited impact on black voting figures. However, Kennedy's Voter Education Project increased black voter registration by over a third. Further to this, the Voting Rights Act of 1965 increased black voter registration across the USA by 2 million. Consequently, more black people were elected to government positions in the North. For example, Robert C. Henry became Mayor of Springfield, Ohio, in 1966 - the first African American city mayor. Changes in voter registration were less marked in the southern states. Although there was an increase of 230,000 in black voter registration in the South between 1965 and 1966, by 1966, 4 out of 13 southern states still had fewer than half of their black citizens registered to vote. In this way, while black Americans were guaranteed equal voting rights to white Americans, in practice, many black Americans in the southern states felt unable to take advantage of these rights.

EXAMINER COMMENT

This paragraph uses well-selected information to present a balanced analysis. The impact of low voter registration on other aspects of life could have been developed. For example, without political representation, it was difficult for black Americans to put pressure on the government to uphold its commitment to racial equality.

In terms of employment and income, there was a definite improvement during the 1960s but full equality was not achieved. Government initiatives throughout the period attempted to ensure fair employment practices. The culmination of these was the Civil Rights Act of 1964, which explicitly outlawed racial discrimination in employment. However, these initiatives did not lead to racial equality. By 1963, black unemployment was 11 per cent - twice the national unemployment level, and by 1965 the income of black workers was only 53 per cent the national average income. By 1968 there were signs of improvement. Black unemployment levels had fallen to 7 per cent, compared to national figures of 5 per cent. However, conditions were still poor in urban areas, prompting the Black Panthers to set up the 'Free Meals for School Children' campaign in 1968. Overall, by 1968 significant de jure steps had been taken towards racial equality in employment. However, these measures were difficult to enforce and consequently their effects had been limited.

EXAMINER COMMENT

This paragraph is clearly focused on the question and discusses a series of legal and practical factors. The distinction between de jure and de facto progress shows the candidate is thinking analytically.

Turning to housing, there was substantially less improvement. In 1960 the census showed that the quality of housing for black Americans was low. For example, 46 per cent of black Americans lived in housing that was unsafe, and 25 per cent of black Americans were living in cramped accommodation. Furthermore, 'white flight' ensured that many black Americans continued to live in areas that were exclusively black. Government initiatives to address these problems had little effect. The 1964 Civil

Rights Act tried to end discrimination in housing but applied to only 1.5 million of the 65 million homes in America. The 1968 Fair Housing Act prohibited discrimination in 80 per cent of the housing market but did not include a means of enforcement. These weak measures ensured that housing discrimination continued throughout America and that black Americans did not have equal rights when trying to find a home.

EXAMINER COMMENT

This paragraph is clearly relevant to the question and contains detailed examples. Finally, it reaches a judgement about the extent to which equality had been achieved in terms of housing. Importantly, the judgement is supported by the evidence in the rest of the paragraph.

The 1896 Plessy v. Ferguson case had ruled that it was possible to have segregation and racial equality. However, NAACP court cases in the 1940s and early 1950s overturned this ruling, showing that the two were mutually exclusive. From this point onwards, racial equality had to entail complete desegregation. By 1968 there was no legal basis for racial segregation. The 1964 Civil Rights Act had made all forms of racial segregation illegal, and the 1965 Voting Rights Act had guaranteed black Americans the right to vote. However, this de jure equality was not supported by de facto equality. Racism on the part of the general public and the reluctance of politicians to enforce these new laws ensured that many black Americans continued to experience social and economic prejudice. Additionally, the low number of black voters prevented black Americans from using political power to challenge this discrimination.

EXAMINER COMMENT

The essay is focused, detailed and wide ranging. Additionally, there is a sustained focus on the distinction between *de jure* and *de facto* change, which allows the candidate to consider how far and in what sense racial equality had been achieved. The answer deserves a Level 5 mark (27 out of 30).

Sample answer 2

How far had equality for black Americans been achieved by 1968?

An answer given a mark in Level 3 of the published mark scheme

The civil rights campaigners used many methods to campaign for racial equality by 1968. They used peaceful protest such as boycotts and sit-ins to draw attention to the fact that segregation laws were unfair. In addition, they used marches and speeches to get support for the movement. They believed that if they had enough support, the government would have no choice but to end segregation and bring about racial equality.

EXAMINER COMMENT

This is not a strong introduction. It is answering a different question from the one set. Instead of focusing on the extent to which racial equality had been achieved, it focuses on how the civil rights movement hoped to achieve equality.

In 1955 Martin Luther King launched the Montgomery Bus Boycott. For a year, black residents of Montgomery refused to use the buses, and instead they walked to work or used car pools. As a result, the bus companies in Montgomery lost a great deal of their income. The media became interested in the protest and people all around the world were able to see pictures of the protest. This gained support for the civil rights movement. At the same time as the protest, a court case called Browder v. Gayle was fought by the NAACP. In December 1956, as a result of this court case, the segregation of buses was declared unconstitutional, and the buses in Montgomery were ordered to desegregate. This was a large step towards racial equality as now black people could sit anywhere they wanted to on a bus and did not have to give up their seats to white people. A previous court case, Morgan v. Virginia in 1946, had already ruled that interstate transport should be desegregated, so by 1968, racial equality had been achieved in all transport.

EXAMINER COMMENT

There is some relevant focus here. The student explains the achievements of early campaigns for the desegregation of transport and links these to the question. However, this link is simplistic, with an assumption that legal equality meant equality in practice.

Racial equality was also achieved in terms of education. Following the case Brown v. Board of Education, all schools had to be desegregated. This led to an increase in the number of children in desegregated schools. However, because no firm timeframe was agreed, many children remained in segregated schools. Later, the Higher Education Act provided money to support poorer children - many of whom were black - through higher education. This resulted in lots more black students going to college or university. Overall, these measures meant that by 1968, black students had the right - and the resources - to an education equal to that of white students.

EXAMINER COMMENT

This paragraph is focused on the question and reaches a clear judgement about the extent of racial equality in education. However, the examples provided to support this argument lack detail. The dates of the court cases are not mentioned and there are no statistics to show how many students attended desegregated schools or progressed to higher education.

By 1968, racial equality had not been achieved in terms of voting rights. Eisenhower introduced two Civil Rights Acts that focused on voting rights. He aimed to increase the number of black Americans who were registered to vote. However, his Acts were weak, and by 1963 only 3 per cent more black voters had been added to the voting registers. Later, President Kennedy introduced his Voter Education Project. This gave government support to activists from SNCC and CORE to help them to recruit black voters. This project increased the number of black registered voters by 260,000.

EXAMINER COMMENT

This paragraph is focused on the question and includes detailed examples. Nonetheless, it fails to mention the Voting Rights Act of 1965. This Act was fundamental to improving black voter registration, and as a result the conclusions drawn here cannot represent the true picture. A better paragraph would also draw explicit links between this evidence and the question, reaching a judgement about how far racial equality had been achieved.

Overall, by 1968 black Americans did have racial equality. Segregation was illegal, and the government could enforce desegregation. In addition, black Americans were earning more than they had before and black unemployment levels had fallen.

EXAMINER COMMENT

This conclusion does not reflect the conclusions drawn earlier in the essay. Throughout the answer, evidence has been provided to show that racial equality did not exist in 1968. However, the student has disregarded this in the conclusion. In addition, the student introduces a new point – about income and employment – in the conclusion, rather than developing this in the main body of the essay. For these reasons, it is a weak conclusion.

This essay is generally focused on the question and is quite detailed. It also discusses racial equality in three areas: transport, education and voting rights. This essay would achieve a Level 3 mark (17 out of 30). It could be improved by a better focus on the question and more specific detail. In order to get into Level 4 it would also need to include explicit evaluation which directly addresses how far racial equality had been achieved.

Index

Published by Pearson Education Limited, a company incorporated in England and Wales, having its registered office at Edinburgh Gate, Harlow, Essex, CM20 2JE. Registered company number: 872828

Edexcel is a registered trademark of Edexcel Limited

Text © Pearson Education Limited 2009

First published 2009
12 11 10 09
10 9 8 7 6 5 4 3 2

British Library Cataloguing in Publication Data
A catalogue record for this book is available from the British Library

ISBN 9781846903069

Project management by the Cambridge Editorial Partnership, www.camedit.com
Edited by Caroline Low
Typeset by Ian Foulis
Original illustrations © Pearson Education 2009
Printed in Malaysia, CTP-KHL

Acknowledgements
The author and publisher would like to thank the following individuals and organisations for permission to reproduce photographs:
Bettmann pp 9, 13, 28, 30, 51, 61, 72, 82, 111; Corbis/Flip Schulke front cover; Corbis p 108; Harry S. Truman Library p 19; Jack Moebes p 38; Flip Schulke p 75; Steve Schapiro p 44; Lief Skoogfors p 103; Miroslav Zajíc p 87

The author and publisher would like to thank the following individuals and organisations for permission to reproduce copyrighted material:
Quote on p 18 from Harry S. Truman from the 1940 congressional election speech, source: Public Papers of the Presidents, which is available in book format and in various on-line sources including the Truman Library's website, http://www.trumanlibrary.org/ publicpapers/index.php; quotes and diagram on pp 19 and 20 from *To Secure These Rights*, the report of the President's Committee on Civil Rights, published in 1947. http://www.trumanlibrary.org/civilrights/srights1.htm#contents, source: Harry S. Truman Library and Museum; extract on p 20 from Executive Order 9981, signed by President Truman in June 1948, source: Harry S. Truman Library and Museum; quotes on pp 68–72 and 87 by Malcolm X, including 'The Ballot or the Bullet' speech, 1964, reproduced with permission by CMG Worldwide; quote on p 80 from Huey Newton, copyright © The Blank Panther Foundation; and extract on p 80 from *The Black Panthers Ten-Point Programme*, published 15 October 1966, copyright © The Blank Panther Foundation.

Every effort has been made to contact copyright holders of material reproduced in this book. Any omissions will be rectified in subsequent printings if notice is given to the publishers.

Websites
The websites used in this book were correct and up to date at the time of publication. It is essential for tutors to preview each website before using it in class so as to ensure that the URL is still accurate, relevant and appropriate. We suggest that tutors bookmark useful websites and consider enabling students to access them through the school/college intranet.

Disclaimer
This material has been published on behalf of Edexcel and offers high-quality support for the delivery of Edexcel qualifications. This does not mean that the material is essential to achieve any Edexcel qualification, nor does it mean that it is the only suitable material available to support any Edexcel qualification. Edexcel material will not be used verbatim in setting any Edexcel examination or assessment. Any resource lists produced by Edexcel shall include this and other appropriate resources.

Copies of official specifications for all Edexcel qualifications may be found on the Edexcel website: www.edexcel.com